Robert Payne Smith

Daniel

An exposition of the historical portion of the writings of the prophet Daniel

Robert Payne Smith

Daniel

An exposition of the historical portion of the writings of the prophet Daniel

ISBN/EAN: 9783337037406

Printed in Europe, USA, Canada, Australia, Japan

Cover: Foto ©Lupo / pixelio.de

More available books at **www.hansebooks.com**

DANIEL:

An Exposition

OF THE

HISTORICAL PORTION OF THE WRITINGS OF THE PROPHET DANIEL.

BY THE

VERY REV. R. PAYNE SMITH, D.D.

DEAN OF CANTERBURY

LONDON:
JAMES NISBET & CO., 21 BERNERS STREET.
MDCCCLXXXVI.

PREFATORY NOTE.

The papers of which this work is composed will be recognised by some readers as having already appeared in a serial form. As they were written at intervals, there is in them a certain amount of repetition, though less than I feared would be the case when they were gathered for publication in a more connected form. They lay claim to no great originality or research, nor do they attempt more than to give a passing glance at some of the difficulties suggested in modern times with regard to a book so marvellous in its contents. They were written rather with a view to edification, and in the hope of drawing from the narrative lessons for our own conduct and guidance in the Christian life. They are reissued at the instance of the Editor of the *Homiletic Magazine*, who insists that there is in the papers, not only " much information conveyed in a popular form, but many suggestions such as will be useful to preachers and Christian workers, as yet unreached by that theological periodical." I therefore only yield to his earnest wish in now sending them forth in this volume.

R. PAYNE SMITH.

Deanery, Canterbury,
September 1886.

CONTENTS.

	PAGE
I. INTRODUCTORY	1
II. DANIEL AND HIS FRIENDS	19
III. SUCCESSIVE MONARCHIES	37
IV. THE DREAM OF NEBUCHADNEZZAR	54
V. A CONSTRAINED CONFESSION	70
VI. THE DURA IMAGE	84
VII. THE ACCUSATION	99
VIII. CALMNESS AND FURY	118
IX. THREE JEWISH CONFESSORS	133
X. HEATHEN RECOGNITION OF GOD	147
XI. A WATCHER AND A HOLY ONE	159
XII. THE ASTONIED INTERPRETER	171
XIII. THE ROYAL PENITENT	185
XIV. BELSHAZZAR THE KING	201
XV. THE HANDWRITING ON THE WALL	214
XVI. AN UNWELCOME EXPLANATION	227

		PAGE
XVII.	MENE, MENE .	242
XVIII.	THE FALL AND RISE OF EMPIRES	258
XIX.	THE HOUR OF DANGER .	273
XX.	THE NEMESIS OF FLATTERY .	286
XXI.	THE RIGHTEOUS DELIVERED .	299
XXII.	RIGHTEOUS RETRIBUTION .	318

DANIEL.

I.

INTRODUCTORY.

THE Book of Daniel holds so remarkable a place in the cycle of Holy Scripture that it seems necessary, before using it for homiletic purposes, to point out a few of its distinctive characteristics.

First, then, and chief of all, prophecy in the Book of Daniel ceases to be Jewish and becomes Gentile. Up to this time, though the prophets with one consent had declared the catholicity of the religion of the Messiah, yet the outward form, under which they had depicted its universality, had in the main been that of the triumph of Judaism and of the one God over the motley idols of the heathen world. The Messiah was to inaugurate a universal empire of peace, but as the Jew read the flowing metaphors and images under which it was set forth, it seemed to him to foreshow the conquest of the world by a Prince of

A

David's line; and their scribes, holding this as a settled truth, eagerly discussed the further question as to the continuance of this Prince's reign. Was it to be indefinitely prolonged? and how in that case was His life to be maintained beyond the age allotted to man? Naturally this was their interpretation of the words of their prophets. For the ideas, the metaphors, the whole of the outward form, was taken either from the Mosaic dispensation, or from the great development of Judaism in David's time, of which the service and ritual of the Temple was the symbol. But while in the prophecies of Daniel the inner core is the same, the outer aspect is completely changed. Still there is a universal empire, but it is a stone cut without hands out of a mountain, and following upon mighty Gentile kingdoms, whose work it does, whereas they had failed. For theirs had been but a temporary rule, while that of the final kingdom would be eternal. As the Jew compared the prophecies of Daniel with those of Isaiah, he must have wondered at the omission in the words of the Babylonian seer of all reference to the part which Israel was to take in the subjugation of the world to God. Isaiah had described his people as being specially the "servant of Jehovah," His prime minister and vizier in the accomplishment of His eternal purpose. In Daniel the Jew falls entirely out of the scene. It was a most necessary lesson, though a hard and painful one for the poor exiles to learn; but this widening and enlarging of the outlook of prophecy was indispensable, and the time had come when it could be no longer delayed. We probably have but half fathomed the full effects of the Babylonian exile in the preparation for Christ's Advent. But we can easily see that, as a fact, at Babylon prophecy broke through the narrow shell which had previously enclosed it, and took wider and more vast dimensions. And this was the result of providential arrangements— made, we may feel sure, for this very end. The one purpose with which all ancient history was instinct was Christ's coming. It appears dimly but certainly in the histories of Greece and Rome; more plainly in those of Egypt and the mighty monarchies whose seats were on the Tigris and Euphrates; with unveiled clearness in the history of the Jews. But we must now confine ourselves to the circumstances which exerted their influence upon Daniel's mind, and enabled him to shake off so completely the narrower feelings natural to those brought up among the exclusive views and tenets which prevailed at Jerusalem.

We find, then, that Daniel, who was probably of

the king's seed (ch. i. 3), was carried captive to Babylon in the third year of the reign of Jehoiakim. Jeremiah (ch. xxv. 1) describes it as the fourth year, counting by the dates of the years; but as three full years had not passed away since Jehoiakim's accession, there is no real disagreement between the two records. Nebuchadnezzar, who at that time was not the king, but only associated with his father, Nabopolassar, in the government of the Babylonian empire, marched early in the year to meet Pharaoh-Necho, who had invaded his dominions, and defeated him at Carchemish on the river Euphrates. The Egyptian king had started four years previously for this trial of strength, determined, if he could, to crush this rising Babylonian power in its youth, and win for himself universal empire. But Josiah, king of Judah, had felt himself bound to resist his progress, and though the battle terminated in his defeat and death, yet was the fight so stubborn that Pharaoh had to return to his own land to recruit his strength. What might have been the result had Josiah let the Egyptian army go unmolested on its way we cannot tell; but certainly the Babylonians would not have had the presence of Nebuchadnezzar, whose genius subsequently won for his country its short-lived empire. As it was, the struggle was delayed for four years, and ended in the disastrous defeat of the Egyptian army.

Nebuchadnezzar pursued it only as far as " the river of Egypt," the brook which formed the boundary between the Philistine country and the territory of the Egyptians. For on his way tidings reached him of his father's death; and, as there were many of the nobles of Babylon ready to contest with this new dynasty the throne of their country, he hastened back to secure for himself the crown. But on his march homewards he made a short halt at Jerusalem to secure the allegiance of Jehoiakim, who had been placed upon the Jewish throne by Pharaoh-Necho, and regarded himself doubtless as his vassal. Jehoiakim seems even to have made some show of resistance, and was at all events treated as a conquered foe, and had to pay the victor a tribute both of captives and of treasures. For the latter he gave some of the choice vessels of the Temple, precious both for their material, and still more for their archaic workmanship; for the former, youths chiefly members of the royal family and of noble houses, who would both adorn Nebuchadnezzar's court, and also serve as hostages for the fidelity of their nation.

Of these Daniel was one, and being selected on account of his beauty and ability for special training, he was brought up not as a Jew, but as a Gentile; not in the house of any of his own people, but under Chaldean teachers and schoolmasters. His education was not such as he would have had in one of the schools of the prophets, but was in the Chaldean language and literature, embracing no doubt the cuneiform system of writing, and the Accadian as well as the ordinary Semitic language. He would become, of course, deeply versed in their system of divination, both by means of the stars and by traditional rules for the interpretation of dreams. Upon this part of Daniel's education Mr. Lenormant has thrown great light by his work on "Magic as Practised by the Chaldeans," published in French at Paris in 1874. He would learn also their venerable liturgies and hymns, addressed to the powers of nature as divine, to the sun, and earth, and sky, the ocean and the wind, and, above all, to fire. Better than all, he would learn astronomy, in the study of which the Chaldeans, blessed with a bright, clear atmosphere, greatly excelled. All this would be a new and marvellous world to the young Jew, and, with its strange admixture of truth and error, of real knowledge and childish superstition, could not but have a powerful influence upon his mind.

As far as we can calculate, Daniel was about

fourteen or fifteen years old when his education began in knowledge of which so much has in the last few years been recovered for us by the deciphering of the cuneiform inscriptions. From the second chapter we learn that this training began immediately after he had been made a captive, and, as the Jewish monarchy had eighteen years of slow wasting and decay to pass through between that third year of Jehoiakim and the fall of Zedekiah, its last weak king, Daniel must have reached the prime of manhood, and have held a position of great power and influence at Nebuchadnezzar's court long before Jerusalem perished in the flames. The exiled Ezekiel, in coupling his name with those of Noah and Job (Ezek. xiv. 14), leads us to the conviction that his reputation for goodness and wisdom was spread throughout the whole region wherein the captive Israelites dwelt. It was a merciful provision for them that at the conqueror's court there should be one who could do so much to soften the bitterness of their condition, and whose example would strengthen them so greatly in holding firmly to their faith. But our theme relates rather to the influence which this training must have had upon his own mind, and to the different way in which, consequently, he treats the old familiar subjects of Jewish prophecy.

For before very long he attained to a position of great eminence, wherein new influences were brought to bear upon him which could not but help to mould his character. Nebuchadnezzar had a dream which, while it greatly startled him, yet passed away entirely from his memory; and when the Chaldeans could tell the king neither the interpretation, nor, what was confessedly beyond their art, the dream itself, he ordered all the members of the college of wise men to be put to death. The Jewish children were included in the terms of this savage decree, and when Daniel and his companions were sought for that they might be slain, he found favour with the captain of the guard, obtained an audience with the king, and undertook, if time were given him, to declare to him all he wished. The evening he spent in earnest prayer with his three companions, and in a vision of the night the secret was revealed to him. The result was that Nebuchadnezzar made Daniel, young as he was, "a great man, and gave him many great gifts, and made him ruler over the whole province of Babylon, and chief of the governors over all the wise men of Babylon" (ch. ii. 48).

Thus at the early age of sixteen or seventeen Daniel began to feel the pressure of the cares of government, and to be brought into daily contact with people of every class. Not that we are to conclude that Daniel attained at one bound to the high position of chief ruler of the province of Babylon. It is the custom of Holy Scripture to include in such a statement as this the ultimate as well as the immediate results of an event. Daniel was at once admitted into the royal service, and given rank among the wise men; and being thus placed in a position which enabled him to give good proof of his ability and fidelity, his promotion was rapid, and he finally became Nebuchadnezzar's chief minister and the head of the college of sages. Now Babylon was at that time a place of great trade. It was the emporium to which the produce of India—its precious stones and spices, its muslins and cloths, and the cunning work of its artificers—was brought, and thence dispersed far and wide. It was the place to which every year hordes of men, torn from their homes to people the vast solitudes of Nebuchadnezzar's colossal city, were dragged as prisoners of war. It was the headquarters of his army, and the place which he was labouring earnestly to adorn with magnificent buildings as well as to protect with vast fortifications. What a strange variety of business would occupy Daniel's thoughts! What motley races of men would awaken his interest! With what vast designs and purposes would he be made familiar! And what an influence must the genius of Nebuchadnezzar have exerted upon him! He would learn something of the vastness of the world, and of the worth and dignity even of heathen men. While still he loved Jerusalem as the city of God, he would think no scorn of the great capital of the mighty empire wherein he was so highly placed.

Nor was it worldly business alone which occupied him. He was chief ruler of the college of the magi. An alien literature and religion was spread before him, and we may well suppose him endeavouring to clear away from it novel superstitions, and to bring it back to the simple truths which it had received from primeval tradition. Placed as he was at its head, it was his business not to destroy, but to purify; to root out the evil and expand and strengthen the good. And whatever there was in it of truth he would know; for it would keep back none of its esoteric teaching from him. And thus his position was full of anomalies. He was at once a Jewish captive and a Babylonian ruler; an earnest worshipper of Jehovah and the head of a Chaldean college. Who can wonder if, under such influences, he took a larger and wider view of the world's purpose and destiny than he could have done if he had remained an inhabitant of a town so small, but with such strongly-marked features, as Jerusalem?

And this seems to have continued to be Daniel's position throughout Nebuchadnezzar's long reign; but when his son Evil-Merodach was murdered, Daniel withdrew into obscurity. When, some years afterwards, the handwriting came upon the wall, and none could interpret it, the Queen-mother called his long services to mind, and told the degenerate king of the "light and understanding and wisdom" which his father (or rather his grandfather) Nebuchadnezzar had ever found in this faithful Jew. That very night Darius the Mede took the kingdom; and when the history of that banquet, and of the strange scene which occurred in it, was reported to him, Daniel was at once raised to favour. And soon afterwards, when Darius took measures for the good government of the mighty empire he had won, Daniel was made chief of the presidents, and apparently continued to be the prime minister of the Median and Persian rulers till his death.

We have, then, in Daniel a man of intense religious feeling and a pure patriot, and one possessed also of great ability and a powerful mind, upon which numerous and weighty influences were brought to bear. Can we wonder if he viewed the world with a different eye from that of the exiled priest Ezekiel, living in penury among the poor Jewish colonists planted on the river Chebar? or from that of Jeremiah, struggling against all the evil influences which were daily dragging the feeble Zedekiah and the decaying people of Jerusalem down to ruin? or even from that of Isaiah, whose rapt vision, spurning this poor earth, soared aloft to the spiritual glories of Messiah's reign, and sang how the sucker, springing up from Jesse's cut-down lineage, and growing as a root in a dry ground, should by its wounds bring to the world healing, and by its death purchase for mankind life? But each of these had his own office and his special message; and Daniel's office was to show that the Christian religion was not to be an enlarged Judaism, but a Judaism fulfilled and made free. Its outer husk was to fall away, its inner beauty to reveal itself; and, instead of a Church for the Jews, there was to be a Church for all mankind.

In the Book of Daniel we find no trace of that old contempt for the Gentiles which the Jews had grafted upon the feelings, in which they might rightly indulge, of gratitude to God for their own many privileges. Babylon to him is the head of gold; other realms are of silver, or brass, or iron, all precious and enduring substances, though the last was mingled with miry clay. In this colossal image Judea finds no place, because thus far its influence upon the world had been nought. And when God's universal empire grinds to powder these world-powers, though Israel had been God's preparation for the reign of Christ, yet that is passed over, and its establishment is spoken of as God's direct doing—a stone cut out of the mountain by no human hands, but by a Divine power. The thought present to the young Jew's mind is that of the one God establishing one kingdom and one religion on earth, and he sees these world-kingdoms preparing the way for it, but themselves coming to nought as it grows and spreads over all the world. We know how he loved his nation, and how, even in extreme old age, he still prayed with his face towards Jerusalem; but he places out of sight the work of his country and of his Church, and sees only the world's history, and the share which it has in preparing for the universal dominion of God.

As a corrective to the outer form of previous prophecy this was not only most precious, but absolutely necessary. A careless reader up to this time might have supposed that the Gentiles had no part in God's purposes. True that the old promises in the Book of Genesis included them, but as Judaism developed, the Gentiles were pushed more and more into the background, and became the object of prophecy apparently only in their connection with Judea or as the future subjects of Judah's Messiah. We, as we read the words of the prophets, cannot help finding proofs everywhere that what Daniel taught was no new interpretation, but the true meaning of the whole prophetic choir. The Jew saw no such worldwide purpose, not merely because patriotism and national pride closed the avenues of his mind, but also because the outer form of prophecy was Jewish, and gave a basis to the narrow interpretation put upon the prophetic teaching by the current national thought. But here the outer form is entirely changed, and the man who was the mighty pillar of their strength in their days of disaster sets the world before them in a completely different aspect, ignores their old standards of thought, and declares that their Jehovah was as much the God and Father of the whole Gentile world as He was their own. But clear and plain as was his teaching, the Jews refused to it their assent; their synagogue did not include Daniel among the prophets, but placed his book among the Hagiographa, "the sacred writings," between those of Esther and Ezra. Nor was this place so altogether wrong; for even now, with its numerous points of resemblance to the Apocalypse of St. John, it would rightly hold a place beween the Old and the New Testaments. It would be hard indeed to spare Malachi from that position, with his ringing announcement of the nigh coming of the Forerunner. But the Apocalypse holds to the Christian Church the same relation as that held by Daniel to the Church of the Jews. The one raised the veil for the covenant people of old, and gave them an insight into and guidance through the weeks and years that were to elapse before Messiah's first Advent; the second raises the veil for the Church of Christ, and gives it glimpses of the world's history and of God's work in it until its Lord comes again.

A few words remain to be said as to Daniel's method of prophesying. Passing by the opening chapters, in which the imagery is taken from Nebuchadnezzar's dreams, we find him using symbolic figures and symbolic numbers. He discontinues now the use of the Chaldean language, by which he had previously seemed to indicate that his memorial was not addressed to Jews only, but to all the people of the province of Babylon, and writes in Hebrew, the holy and sacred language of his people. But how different his method from that of the prophets of old! Mighty animals devour, and break in pieces, and trample the nations down, till all the thrones of earthly dominion are cast aside, and the Ancient of Days takes the kingdom. So great an influence did this mode of writing exercise upon the imagination of mankind that the books are Legion written by the Jews, especially those of Egypt, in imitation of it. One of the most famous was the Book of Enoch; another, the Second Book of Esdras, may be found in our own Apocrypha, though not included in it by the Church of Rome. It was written by some Jew early in the second century after Christ, and contains in the eleventh chapter a sketch of the twelve Cæsars under the image of an eagle with twelve feathered wings, and may well serve to illustrate the use made in subsequent times of Daniel's method of prophesying. In these visions, and in that of the kings of the north and of the south, the illustration of Gentile history is Daniel's primary object. The Gentiles no longer appear as mere accessories to the Jews; they are equally the object of the Divine providence, and bear an independent, if not an equal, part in the preparation for Christ.

Finally, by symbolic numbers he taught with extraordinary clearness when the Messiah was to come. The day of His Advent is now no longer indefinite or only approximately fixed; it is exactly declared. But with what bitter revelations is it combined! What must have been the Jew's feelings when, instead of triumph and victory, and an era of glorious conquest and universal empire, he read that Messiah was to be cut off, and that the armies of an alien empire would destroy the city and the sanctuary! that the daily sacrifice would cease, and that the abomination that maketh desolate would prevail for one thousand three hundred and ninety days!

This second portion of the Book of Daniel we shall for the present leave untouched; for it requires different and more scholarly treatment than the first. Some of it, indeed, would have to be illustrated by historical and chronological disquisitions of considerable length, though, on the other hand, the prophecies relating to the Messiah and to the general resurrection are inferior to no parts of Holy Scripture, either in interest or in the importance of the lessons which they teach. The book, however, definitely falls into two sections, marked by the different languages in which they are written, each complete in itself, and each contribut-

B

ing in its own way to that transition from Hebrew prophecy to the ideal of the Christian Church which makes the position in the Bible of the whole so unique. It is, then, upon the first six chapters that we propose to give notes for homiletic purposes, in the hope that the manifold lessons which they contain may be more clearly seen, and that the Book of Daniel, instead of being a mere battlefield for criticism, may take its due place in the maintenance among us of a holy and devout life.

II.

DANIEL AND HIS FRIENDS.

(DANIEL i. 1-21).

THE facts are as follow: 1. Jerusalem is temporarily occupied by a Babylonian army, and some of the treasures of the House of Jehovah are carried away and placed in a heathen temple at Babylon. 2. Together with the sacred vessels, some high-born youths are selected for service at Nebuchadnezzar's court. 3. To render them fit for high office, the king orders them to be trained and educated in all the learning of the Chaldees. 4. Among these youths are Daniel and his three friends, Hananiah, Mishael, and Azariah. 5. To denote that henceforward they are to be regarded as Chaldees, their names are changed. 6. Daniel and his friends refuse to partake of the portion supplied to them of the king's meat, and request leave to have pulse and water given them instead for their maintenance. 7. Through God's blessing they obtain permission to make trial of this diet for ten days, at the end of which time they are found fairer in countenance and fatter in flesh than those who had partaken of the king's meat. 8. By their learning, wisdom, and uprightness they gain the king's favour, and Daniel continues high in rank and powerful in influence until the fall of the Babylonian empire.

I. The temporary capture of Jerusalem by Nebuchadnezzar was one of those merciful warnings by which God holds back the wicked from rashly pursuing their own evil ways. God had given Judah a last and most earnest call to repentance in the reign of the good King Josiah; but it appears that the people had set themselves as determinately against the king's reforms and the prophet Jeremiah's teaching, as previously they had resisted Hezekiah and Isaiah. Now it is a law of God's providence that when men harden themselves against correction, He gives them up to their own devices; and so Hezekiah's successor was the fierce persecutor Manasseh, and Josiah was followed by the selfish and unrighteous Jehoiakim (Jer. xxii. 17). In both of these the people had a king like themselves. The failure of Josiah's earnest efforts appears from the immorality rampant at Jerusalem (Jer. vii. 9), at the very time when the inhabitants were glorying in the restoration of the Temple service (*ibid.* ver. 4); and from the general worship of the Queen of Heaven, the moon-goddess (*ibid.* ver. 18), to which they were so wedded, that even after the fall of Jerusalem the refugees in Egypt ascribed their misfortunes to the anger of this deity for their supposed neglect of her rites (Jer. xliv. 18). It is thus plain that the king's restoration of the Mosaic ritual had not been accompanied either by moral amendment or true allegiance to Jehovah; and that the popular approval of Josiah's acts was dictated, not by real piety, but by superstition. But while the people of Judah were, as a mass, sinking daily deeper in the twin-gulfs of immorality and idolatry, there was a remnant in whom the Jewish Church was to live on, and grow in piety and usefulness (Jer. xxiv. 5–7). And for their sake it was that God gave Jerusalem solemn warning by the presence before it of the Babylonian army. God's people read the signs of the times, and what to others are the mere outcome of earthly ambition and political schemings are seen by them to be manifestations of His will, who guides all things by His overruling wisdom. And so this temporary capture of Jerusalem would deepen in their minds the conviction, already impressed upon them by Jeremiah's words, that God was about to deal in judgment with their city and nation. It would lead also to practical results; for, first, they would be somewhat prepared for their own removal to Babylon. Like trees made ready for transplantation, they would have all the deep roots that bound them to their homes cut through, and so when their turn for going into exile came, it would not be the violent uprooting of men who had been living in security and unprepared. It would be the fulfilling of expectations sad and painful, but of which they had long seen the certainty. And next, the removal of these youths, comparatively few in number, but chosen for their high birth and great natural gifts, was a merciful act intended for the well-being of the Jews when soon afterwards Babylon became their home. When seven more years had passed, the son of Jehoiakim, with the queen-mother and a numerous array of nobles and choice men and artificers, were forced to depart from Jerusalem and take up their abode in the roomy solitudes which Nebuchadnezzar had enclosed within the walls of his capital; and already Daniel and his friends were there, high in office, valued and esteemed; and for their sakes their compatriots would be treated kindly. Under so great a trial, too, when in their misery men's hearts might well give way to despair, the example of Daniel's piety would go far to encourage them.

They would feel that God had not forsaken His people. The conquest of Nebuchadnezzar utterly crushed and obliterated many nations. Judah gained new life from the exile; and this we must ascribe to the combined teaching of Jeremiah, the prophet of woe, and of Daniel, the prime minister of the conqueror, whose position and example alike inspired them with hope, and with the conviction that, in accordance with Jeremiah's prophecy, they would, at the end of seventy years, be restored to their home and country.

We see, then, in this capture of the holy city, first, a warning, rejected by the mass of the people, but heeded by the "remnant," God's chosen few; and, secondly, a preparation for the maintenance of the Church at Babylon, an encouragement to hope, and an alleviation of distress.

We may notice in ver. 1 an interesting fact. The capture of Jerusalem is here said to have been in the *third* year of Jehoiakim; in Jer. xxv. 1 it is called his *fourth*. Both statements are absolutely true; for Jehoiakim at this time had not been king for full thirty-six months, though he had entered upon the fourth year of his reign by the calendar. But Assyriologers tell us that the custom at Nineveh and Babylon was to continue the name of the dead king in the dating of documents till the end of the year, and not to use the name of his successor till New Year's day. Surely it is wonderful how, with increased knowledge, all those little difficulties with which students of the Bible used to be twitted pass away, or even become proof of the genuineness of these holy records. For while Jeremiah at Jerusalem follows the Jewish method of dating, the scribe at Babylon follows the custom prevalent there.

As regards "the vessels of the house of God," we may notice how things set apart for God's service are rejected by Him when they no longer minister to the Divine honour. Those vessels had been the gifts of piety; they may have aided in waking up reverent thoughts in the hearts of generations of worshippers, and in impressing them with a sense of God's majesty and glory. But when the outward service of God became separated from true heartfelt piety, they ceased to be of use, and God let them go into captivity. When the ark was captured and placed in an idol temple, the Philistine fish-god was broken before it (1 Sam. v. 4); but no miracle happens now. Quietly, without let or hindrance, the solemn procession of Chaldee warriors carries these vessels in triumph to the temple of Bel-Merodach. Nothing occurs to mar their rejoicing. No sign is manifested of Jehovah's displeasure. The vessels have become in God's sight as nothing. Why the difference? Because when the ark was captured men had faith, though feeble; and the miracle was wrought to strengthen their feebleness under sore trial. No miracle is ever wrought to aid men who have no faith. And if it were wrought they would not heed it (St. Luke xvi. 31). At Babylon miracles were wrought for the sake of the believers there: for these corrupt Jews of Jerusalem none. A miracle for them would have strengthened them in superstition; just as of old it would have produced the same effect upon the Israelites, if the ark, ministered to by immoral priests, had won for them victory.

II. With merciful warning and deserved punishment for the guilty people of Jerusalem is joined the hard fate of innocent and pious youths. Unpolluted by the wickedness among which they live, they must yet leave their homes and go into captivity. But first, God's judgments fall upon men by the operation of what seem to us to be natural laws, and in plague, or pestilence, or famine, or war, all share the misery alike (Luke xiii. 1–5). Many wholesome results follow from this, and a constant miraculous intervention to rescue the pious from bearing their part in national or other trials would only weaken and degrade faith. Moreover, trials have a twofold issue. The bad are punished by them; the good urged on to higher degrees of holiness. Daniel might have remained a person of ordinary piety at Jerusalem; he attained to an extraordinary degree of holiness by the purifying and ennobling effects of trouble rightly borne. Again, he was wanted at Babylon. God placed him there to be of use. He was to be the strength and support of all pious Israelites during the seventy years of exile. And God sent others with him—notably his three friends—to be a solace and a comfort to him, as he was for them a defence and protection. When we read Jeremiah's high commendations of the small band of exiles dwelling at Babylon while Jerusalem was still standing, we can well understand the Divine purpose in the removal of Daniel from his home, and how great was the good for others purchased by his personal suffering (Jer. xxiv. 5–7; xxix. 10–14), and the benefit even to himself.

III. As regards the selection and training of these youths, we may notice, first, the pride of the conqueror. He commands his chief chamberlain to choose attendants for him, "both from among the king's seed and also from the nobles." In this was fulfilled the mournful prediction made to

Hezekiah, that children of his issue should serve as eunuchs in the palace of the king of Babylon (Isa. xxxix. 7). For, though we must not place too much confidence in the assertion of Josephus that Daniel was a son of Zedekiah, undoubtedly he was of the royal race. But, secondly, after Nebuchadnezzar's pride had been satisfied, all the rest is most wise. The children selected, besides their high birth and handsome persons, are to possess both physical and intellectual vigour. "Skilful in all wisdom," means having an aptitude for acquiring and understanding the knowledge taught in books. They were also to be "knowers of knowledge and able to understand thoughts;" that is, to powerful memories, an important quality in old time when writing was a painful art, they were to add quickness of perception. Such youths after three years' training (ver. 5) would be fit to stand, after the manner of officials and ministers, in the court of the king.

IV. Among those chosen were some whose hearts God had specially touched. Young as they were, the troubles through which they had passed had wrought upon them both for moral and for spiritual good. But how strange are the workings of God's providence! Up to this time they had been trained in that noble learning, which, from the time of Samuel, had been the glory of the prophetic schools. Now they were to be trained in that strange heathen learning, so wonderfully disentombed in our days. Magic, and the interpretation of dreams and omens, formed an important part of this knowledge; and there were, besides, liturgies, hymns, and histories. Up to this time the documents discovered at Babylon have been mostly of a religious character, while among those found at Nineveh and other Assyrian cities have been historical documents of priceless value. To Jewish youths much of this heathen literature must have been repulsive; it must have offended their religious ideas, and often shocked their moral sense. It had nevertheless a good side. It taught them how large the world is, and that God's empire extendeth over all, and that all are objects of His care. Possibly coming before them with the charm of novelty, it may have made them pursue their studies with the same eagerness, and zeal, and curiosity which have spurred on scholars to recover the interpretation of the Sanscrit language, and to decipher these very cuneiform inscriptions in which Daniel and his friends were to have their training. And in thus enlarging their mental vision, God was preparing them to do service for His Church at a time when it was no longer hidden away among the mountains of Judea, but in danger of being trampled under foot in the highway of the nations, and crushed into a shapeless ruin amid the turmoil of uprooted men, and of unsettled thoughts, and of torn-up faiths and convictions, which must have made the social state of Babylon most unhappy, most corrupting, and depressed with the dulness of despair. For what strength for good would men have, dragged from their homes, to be serfs and vassals in the city of those who had destroyed all that they held most dear?

V. And as if to show that they had lost all, the chief chamberlain gives the four youths new names. They were probably about fourteen years of age, and after three years' training would be seventeen, the usual period of life at which men were admitted to serve as attendants at Oriental courts. They were thus of an age when they could understand the full measure of their degradation. High-born, and full of that earnest patriotism which distinguished the Jew, they were to lose the names which told them of Judah's God, and to bear titles of idolatrous significance. In this they had no choice. But though the king could change their names, he could not change their hearts. Young as they were, deprived of their former religious training and privileges, obliged to study heathen lore and have their minds filled with heathen ideas, separated too from Jehovah's worship, and doubtless compelled to take their part in many a heathen festival, God's grace proved sufficient for them, and in the unkindly soil of Babylon they grew up as trees of Jehovah's planting.

VI. For, compelled to yield to much that was most painful to them, yet where they had a choice, Daniel and his three friends determined to abide by Jehovah's law. Daniel must have proved himself docile and affectionate; for otherwise he would not have been brought into "favour and tender love with the prince of the eunuchs" (ver. 9). We see, then, God's watchful care for Daniel. He had not forgotten him, but gave him opportunities of winning the affection of his master. We see also Daniel's loving nature. Wronged and injured, he nevertheless showed himself kind and gentle, and ready to do service for those among whom his lot was cast. We note also his prudence. Where he had no choice he made no resistance. He may have hated his heathenish name, may have disliked and grieved over much which he had to learn; but none of these things were absolutely sinful. It would even be useful for him to understand the nature of the religious ideas and worship of the heathen, provided only that he was allowed to stand apart from the practice of their impurities. He would have to combat heathenism, and to keep his compatriots pure from it; and he must study it, just as a missionary has to study the religion of those whom he hopes to convert. As regards, however, the food supplied for them, Daniel and his friends had here an opportunity of maintaining their Judaism. The king's command was that the young nobles under training should have an allowance of choice food and wine from his table. Now this had become impure in the eyes of a religious Jew by the custom of offering a portion of the meat and pouring out a libation of the wine to some god. To partake of it, therefore, was in some sort to join in heathen worship. Could a worshipper of the one God thus take part, even indirectly, in idolatry? We find the same scruples among the early Christians, and St. Paul commanded the Corinthians not to partake of the flesh of any victim offered in sacrifice (1 Cor. x. 28), because by so doing they became "partakers of the table of devils."

We gather that this was the objection of Daniel and his friends from the nature of the food selected by them. No portion was offered to the gods of any vegetable diet; and thus they reject the wine permitted by the Levitical law, and will eat only of such things as were not tainted by idolatry. Now this refusal might have exposed them to death. They were offering insult to the king's gods, and acting as though the food from the royal table were polluted and impure. But God gave them favour in the sight of the chief chamberlain, and he thought only of their appearance. Regarding their rejection of the food as a boyish scruple, which would soon pass away, and personally fond of Daniel, his only fear was lest the king should notice that their faces were meagre and their beauty diminished, and should order him to be beheaded for not taking proper care of those in training for royal service. But what a picture is this of the ways of men where true religion does not exist! For an act of considerate kindness a faithful officer may lose his life! It is only where the one God is rightly worshipped that true freedom and equal justice can exist. It is not merely for the future world that religion is good; all that is best in human society now God bestows with the knowledge of Himself; and if men reject His reasonable service, with religion all good things will decay and finally come to an end.

VII. Daniel and his friends acknowledge that the risk is a real one, but pray that a ten days' trial may be allowed them. Their faith is strong and earnest. Let but the experiment be made, and they doubt not that God will bless it. And the result answers to their expectations. At the end of the appointed time none were so fair, and sound, and healthy as these four abstemious youths. God's blessing had rested upon their faith; but probably their cheerfulness under trial had also contributed to the result. Faith often brings success by the firmness, security, and peace it gives to the soul. The man who trusts in God faces danger calmly, bears troubles and sorrows with patience, and submits to ill-treatment with resignation. Thus difficulties meet him already half conquered. It is when men kick against the pricks that trial brings anguish. These four pious children, in the midst of cruel wrongs and painful difficulties, were so upheld by faith, that instead of fretting they were peaceful and happy, contented with the heartfelt assurance that in their God they had a friend who would order all things for their good.

VIII. Finally, after the manner of Jewish history, we have a short summary of the fortunes of these four Jewish children during the continuance of the Babylonian empire. What soothsayer would have dared to tell the victorious monarch of the mightiest realm upon earth that one at least of the children whom he was training for his service would live to see his empire come to an end, and would be the prime minister in the kingdom of his vanquisher? Still less would one have dared to tell him that he, the head of gold, would be overthrown, in order that a people few in number, and powerless in earthly strength, might be delivered from Babylon and restored to their land, and that they would found a universal and enduring dominion (Dan. ii. 44). But such was the will of Him who rules over all the kingdoms of the earth, and whose servant Nebuchadnezzar was, raised up for special work (Jer. xxv. 9), though he himself knew not of it.

We see, then, first, God's universal empire, by which He orders the kingdoms of this world for His own high purposes, and raises up rulers and throws them down, not capriciously and without reason, but as the Divine purpose, for which this world was created and constituted such as it is, requires. Next we see His superintending providence watching over His own people. Though they be but a little flock, yet all things are ordered for their sakes, and at one time chastisement, and at another deliverance and mercies, are meted out to them as best may suit their spiritual needs, and the making them fit to be God's messengers to mankind, bearing to a sick world healing, to the fallen recovery, to the fainting hope and strength. Lastly, we see how, amid these general laws, through and by which God works, there is also special care taken of individuals. God's working is so perfect that the government of the world and of nature by general laws does not necessitate individual neglect. There was not only special care for the Jews, as a whole, at Babylon, but special care for Daniel and his three friends. Their faith was not unheeded, nor was their fate left to chance. When Nebuchadnezzar ordered Jewish youths to be chosen for service at his court, he was probably following a not uncommon practice. As nation after nation lost its freedom before his conquering armies, choice youths of royal and princely rank were probably always selected from among the prisoners of war for the king's employ. In this single case it raises up for a remarkable nation one whose business it will be to strengthen its faith and revive its piety, and prevent its absorption into the mass of heathenism among which its lot was for the time cast. And this nation is remarkable simply because it has a mission, a special work to do for God. This youth and his friends make a noble stand for their religion, and find favour with the officer to whose charge they are intrusted.

Instead of a rough answer bidding them submit, he grants, at great personal risk, what may have seemed to him a perverse and unwise whim. But they thrive on the poor fare they have chosen, and make such progress in Chaldean learning and science, and are so aided by the direct blessing and intervention of the Deity in their behalf, that they become high officers of state, possessed of great influence and power, and stand even foremost in the management of the affairs of a mighty empire. No doubt that integrity of character which made them true to their religion gained for them also the king's confidence when he found them upright and incorruptible in their management of his affairs. Many a king since those days has endured ministers whose religion he disliked, because he found them faithful; Daniel's services often won from Nebuchadnezzar favour even for his religion. But it was not simply to his personal worth and usefulness that Daniel owed his influence with the king. It was God's blessing which made him find favour; and this he had because he was a man of faith, of piety, and of prayer.

III.

SUCCESSIVE MONARCHIES.

(DANIEL ii. 1–30.)

THE facts of Nebuchadnezzar's vision are these: 1. He has a dream which he forgets. 2. He sends nevertheless for the learned men of Babylon, and commands them to tell him not only the interpretation, but the dream itself. 3. They expostulate with him on the unreasonableness of his requirement, but in vain; and he commands them to be put to death. 4. Daniel and his companions, who were included in this cruel decree, ask for an audience, and promise that if time be granted them they will fulfil the king's demands. 5. After prayer the secret is revealed to Daniel in a night vision. 6. He is brought into the king's presence, tells the king his dream and interprets it, and with his companions is raised to high rank in the kingdom of Babylon.

I. The dream of Nebuchadnezzar happened in "the second year of his reign" as sole monarch, after the death of his father Nabopolassar, and thus about four years after Daniel and his friends had commenced their training. As this was to last three years (chap. i. 5), they would have been initiated in all the secrets of the wise men, and admitted into their college about twelve months before this crisis came, and would thus be ready to occupy, as the result of their success, a position wherein they would be able to render most important services to their countrymen when brought captives to Babylon. Nebuchadnezzar, moreover, would be now fully established upon the throne, with all rivals crushed, and be able to take to heart the lessons of the dream. Thus at the very beginning of his reign he would be favourably affected towards the Jews and the God whom they worshipped.

As soon, then, as he was in assured possession of the kingdom, he has a dream sent him by God; that is, being still a heathen, and a man of violent and cruel temperament, he is made the means of a communication from Heaven to earth; and is not only the subject of prophecy, as in Jer. xxv., but has a revelation made to himself, embracing within it not the fortunes only of earthly empires, but also of Christ's kingdom. But prophecy is a gift from without, and is not dependent upon human character. The worldly-minded Balaam may bring God's message and utter it as clearly as the unselfish and devoted Jeremiah. As a message to the heart, its influence will largely depend upon the character of the bearer, and God's prophets have, as a rule, been "men of whom the world was not worthy." But there are times when God uses the unrighteous for righteous purposes; and thus He employed the tyrant king of Babylon to teach men a great lesson concerning earthly empire.

And so as regards His word now. When the holy message is brought by an unholy man, it is still God's message, and will do God's work. But there can be no fit bringing of that message unless the bearer be one after God's own heart: nor will there be any blessing for the bearer himself. He speaks most powerfully for God who speaks from the heart to the heart. Without this, there is heavy responsibility for the preacher, and many will even be set against the message because of the unworthiness of him who brings it, and the contrast between the pure words sent from Heaven and the speaker's impure lips. But against this we should be upon our guard. The word of God is a message of life to our soul, whatever may be the means used for sending it to us; and we may well believe that during the exile thousands of Jewish hearts were strengthened and their sorrows alleviated by the revelation made to a heathen, and one who was their cruel conqueror. For they learned by it that the kingdom of their Messiah was finally to prevail, to extend over all the earth, and to endure for ever.

And this revelation came in the form of a dream, and it is remarkable that this is generally the manner in which revelations are made to the heathen. Thus in the Book of Genesis it was in a dream that God spake to Abimelech and to Pharaoh. So too in the Book of Judges the onslaught of Gideon upon the camp of the Midianites was foreseen by one of that heathen host in a dream. To his own people, also, God, among many ways, speaks sometimes in dreams, as to Joseph and Solomon: but it is not difficult to understand why this method of communication is the one peculiarly fitting for heathen men and unbelievers. For it does not bring the person communicated with into any direct connection with the Deity. Dreamland is a confused and shadowy region, and what passes there is but faint and indistinct. But in this confused state of thought conscience is often very active, and thus there is frequently a religious character about dreams which made the heathen regard them as Divine. But it was the subsequent interpretation which gave them their value.

Pharaoh's dreams about the kine and the ears of corn would have passed away after a few hours' wonder but for Joseph's interpretation. They were for Joseph's sake, and served to introduce him to the king, and give his person and his word value in Pharaoh's eyes. And so here. These dreams did not come for Nebuchadnezzar's sake. They came for the sake of God's people Israel, and through them for the good of His whole Church. But it was necessary that Nebuchadnezzar should be brought into kindly relations with the Jews, and especially that Daniel should gain influence over him, and that he and other exiles should have places of trust and power which would enable them to protect their countrymen. Liable as they were now to persecution, because in religion they stood alone and refused to take part in the rites of any worship but their own, it was of primary importance that the king should be well affected towards them and their God. And this was naturally the result of the communications made to him, and of the remarkable manner in which Daniel, and he alone, interpreted them.

II. The dream startled the king. He had seen a mighty colossus of bright metals, which suddenly had been smitten by a stone, and had fallen to pieces, while the stone had grown into a mountain. Yet strange as the vision had been, it had left no clear impression upon his mind, but only a vague sense of great terror; and so "his spirit was troubled, and his sleep brake from him." The whole was so ordered as violently to agitate Nebuchadnezzar's feelings. He knew that he was in the presence of extraordinary events; that it was no mere working of his own mind that distressed him: and yet he could recall nothing. Again and again, no doubt, he endeavoured to summon back to memory the visions which had caused his agitation, but they fled from him. It was like the tossing of the sea after a storm. Waves of terror were still surging in his heart; thoughts were chafing one against another; but the cause of all his inward turmoil had passed away, and he could remember nothing of it. And so, wearied with the fruitless inward search, he sent for the wise men of his kingdom, and they came. Confidently perhaps, for they had settled rules by which to interpret dreams, and long experience in the art; and they doubted not but that rich gifts, and high honours, and increased influence over the king's mind would be the reward of the skilful use which they would make of his excitement.

But he had forgotten the dream, and for such a dilemma their art provided them with no expedient. Let the king tell the dream, and they are ready with the interpretation. They had interpreted many a dream before, and sometimes their interpretation had come true, sometimes it had failed, and often had been such as to be capable of more than one explanation. All that was needed was to satisfy the king's mind at the time and quiet his feelings; let a few days pass, and the matter would have lost its importance. But here their claims were subjected to a test, unreasonable if their art was human, reasonable only if they were inspired of God. And when the king urges upon them his demand, accuses them angrily of only wanting to gain time, and threatens them and their families with death unless they make known to him his dream as well as its interpretation, they acknowledge that no magician, or astrologer, or Chaldean could show him what he desired, and that such knowledge belongs to God only.

III. In anger at this opposition to his will, the king commands that all the wise men of Babylon shall be put to death. They formed an important order in the state, and probably as " star-gazers " possessed considerable real knowledge. We find among the cuneiform inscriptions tables of astronomical and astrological observations made in very early times, and constantly added to. The great text-book on these matters, called "The Illumination of Bel," and consisting of seventy-two chapters, was made at least a thousand years before the time of Nebuchadnezzar, and was apparently translated by Berosus into Greek. No doubt there was in it much valuable knowledge: thousands of observations upon the motions of stars and comets, and upon eclipses and strange appearances in the heavens, which would be most precious to our astronomers now. But mixed up with valuable scientific truth was a strange medley of fortune-telling and conjuring. Now it was the large amount of real scientific knowledge possessed by the magi which gave their office its value, and covered their vain pretensions to a knowledge which they did not possess. But at length their empty claims had brought trouble upon them. They had asserted that by their knowledge of the motions of the stars they could foretell the future, and explain dreams and the like. The king had demanded a thing difficult and hard, wherein there was no room for trickery or clever evasion, or answer of dubious meaning. Their knowledge and skill and experience were unequal to the test, and they were condemned to death. Sooner or later, false pretensions are sure to be found out, and to bring trouble on those who have made them.

The decree extended only to the college at

Babylon. There were distinct colleges at Borsippa and elsewhere, but this at Babylon was the head and chief of all. Its members probably were numerous, and many of them had held high rank and enjoyed great favour at court in the days of Nabopolassar. It was a stern and cruel decree. Impostors, as to a great extent they were, yet they did not deserve so harsh a sentence; nor did they even profess to be able to do what the king demanded of them. Still, they had sacrificed truth to falsehood; had claimed for themselves an inspiration which they did not possess; and the time had come when falsehood had failed them, and the emptiness of their professions stood revealed. Deceit never succeeds for more than a limited time. It gains the start, but truth follows upon its track, surely though slowly; and at last deceit finds some obstacle in its way at which it breaks down, and its end is exposure and shame.

IV. But among these impostors were men who were innocent. Daniel and his companions had been trained in Chaldean knowledge; and while rejoicing in much which they learned, had doubtless often grieved over the folly and falsehood which formed the very centre and core of Babylonian astrology. On the one hand, they had been admitted into the vast and general knowledge of men and things which these ancient colleges possessed. In Judea their learning in the prophetic schools had been narrow, but it was true: an intense and earnest doctrine concerning the unity of the nature of God; His universal empire; the emptiness of all claims of idol gods to share His power; the greatness of His love to man; His truth, and justice, and mercy; and His purpose of sending a Messiah for the restoration of mankind, created to be happy in Jehovah's service, but fallen from his high estate,—this was the noble cycle of Jewish knowledge; and, counting this as their true riches the Jews troubled little about the history of heathen nations, or about earthly science and mere secular knowledge. But now Daniel and his companions had been taught much of the history of those mighty kingdoms on the Tigris and Euphrates, which were the first to aspire to universal empire. They had also been taught much science, and especially as to the motions of the planets and the secrets of the star-world; much human knowledge, too, of laws, and manners, and the ways of men had also been communicated to them. On the other hand, their pure minds must have revolted from the unchaste stories of gods and goddesses guilty of flagrant crime; they must have seen with horror licentiousness in its worst forms enshrined in this unholy pantheon of deities devoid of virtue and of shame, and using their power for sins at which men stood aghast. With strangely mingled feelings must they have pursued their studies during their three years' apprenticeship. But their initiation was now over; for some months, possibly, they had even had duties to perform as Chaldeans and soothsayers. God no doubt had spared them from everything that would have degraded them and debased their consciences. We know that He was keeping them for high and holy purposes, and He would guard them from all evil.

Probably they lived much apart. They belonged to a nation accused in old time of being unsocial, and not caring to enjoy the company of their fellow-men. They had too little in common with the members of the college into which they had been admitted; too much that was their own for them to care to mingle much with them. We find that they had not gone with the magi into the king's palace; for we read that "they sought Daniel and his fellows to be slain." They were included in the decree because their training was over; but probably only those who were of foremost rank were summoned to stand before the king. It was hard that they, so young and innocent, should share the fate of those who for so long had enjoyed rank and wealth by the unrighteous use which they made of the weakness and credulity of others. But it was ordered for their good. There must be this deep descent before their rising. There must be fear and terror all around: violent anger on the king's part: danger menacing the wise men: the people excited at the fate which threatened a class whom they regarded as the interpreters of the gods. So would it be clearly shown which was the true God and who was His prophet. And Daniel lost neither his faith nor his presence of mind. For when the news reached him, "he answered with counsel and wisdom," and instead of being hurried to the prison wherein the wise men were collected, as we may suppose, before their execution took place, he is taken into the king's presence, and time is granted him, and a respite for the rest, upon his promising to show the king on the day following his dream and its interpretation.

V. Daniel, we may feel sure, was moved by God to undertake this dangerous office; for dangerous he knew it to be. But he had a resource which these magi did not possess. He believed in the efficacy of prayer. The magi had certain mutterings and repeatings of formal phrases: with Daniel and his companions prayer was the outpouring of the heart to a personal God, the Almighty in heaven. He goes then "to his house," some apartment in the college at Babylon occupied by him in common with the wise men. But while they have only human wisdom and skill, he has an open way to the Giver of all knowledge, and kneeling down with his three friends, they "desire mercies of the God of heaven." When, long afterwards, he was forbidden to pray, we may feel sure that he recalled to mind how prayer in his previous difficulties had saved him. But for prayer he would have been put to death in his early manhood; it had been his strength and comfort throughout a long life beset with countless difficulties and trials. Was he in old age to forego that privilege which in his youth had been the pillar of his safety? No. Yet we may well believe that Daniel prayed upon no calculation: he would equally have prayed had death been its certain result. It was a duty too holy, a privilege too precious, a blessing too transcendent to be lightly abandoned. And at this early date he had probably experienced no other answers to his prayers than such as any believer may receive now. Prayer had not saved him from being dragged away from his home into captivity. It had not rescued him from a mode of life galling and irksome to him. God does not answer prayer in our way It would be dangerous to ourselves and ruinous to others if there were no other element in the answering of prayer than simply the faith of those who pray. A believer would cease to be a man and become a demi-god and a worker of miracles, and the whole constitution of this world be changed, if all that he asked in faith were granted him.

God always answers prayers for the spiritual good of those who pray to Him; but He changes the order of material things and guides the laws of the universe to new results only when a sufficient cause exists for His interference. At Babylon there was such a crisis in the affairs of the Church as made the special manifestation of God's personal presence almost a necessity, if the faith of Israel was to be generally maintained, and the Jewish people return to their land in such a state of mind and in such numbers as would make the restoration of the temporal kingdom possible. And without this our Lord's ministry upon earth would have had no suitable place for its exercise. And thus while Jeremiah wrought no miracles, and while Josiah's pious efforts were strengthened by no supernatural aid, at Babylon miracles were wrought, and God's people there in the fiery furnace of affliction received the heavenly comfort and encouragement which was necessary for them.

And this was the first manifestation of God's presence. Daniel had no reason to expect more help than Jeremiah had received. But he prayed; and he asked others to join him in his prayers. He anticipated the words of our Master where He says, "If two of you shall agree on earth as touching anything that they shall ask, it shall be done for them of My Father which is in heaven." There is a mighty efficacy in united prayer; and when these four youths, lying under sentence of death, joined in supplication, they exercised a power which stormed the battlements of heaven, and obtained for them all they asked.

They prayed "concerning the secret," and "then was the secret revealed to Daniel in a night vision," and he praised and blessed the name of God. In his thanksgiving the leading thought is that God is the real spring and fountain, not only of power but of wisdom. He is not only almighty, but all-wise, a "God of knowledges," as Hannah calls Him (1 Sam. ii. 3), not of one limited and special kind of knowledge, but of knowledge of all and every kind. And, therefore, times and seasons, kings and kingdoms, are in His hand; for His almighty power enables Him to execute all that His wisdom approves.

VI. And now, in full possession of the secret,

Daniel goes to Arioch, and demands an immediate audience of the king. What all their treasures of knowledge could not enable the wise men to unravel had been made plain and easy to this youth. They had stored up treasures of centuries of knowledge. From their lofty observatory in Babylon they had watched every motion of the stars, but no combination of the planets had forewarned them of their danger or suggested a way of escape; and no denizen of the starry world had descended to tell them the dream and its interpretation. They had read, perhaps, and studied "The Illumination of Bel," but had gained thence no light. Twenty-four hours had passed since Nebuchadnezzar had sprung from his startled sleep and summoned them into his council-chamber. They had listened to his demand, had remonstrated and protested, but in vain. And they had given the matter up, and in silent despair awaited the hour of their execution. They knew nothing of prayer; had no loving God to address and obtain help from. Their art had failed them; and their art was all they had.

It is a grand and noble speech which Daniel addresses to the king. "The secret which the king hath demanded cannot the wise men, the astrologers, the magicians, the soothsayers, show unto the king; but there is a God in heaven that revealeth secrets, and maketh known to the king Nebuchadnezzar what shall be in the latter days." He claims no special skill; it is no human wisdom, no illumination from any earthly source, that has taught him what had troubled the king upon his bed in night visions. It was a higher power; a God, not on earth, but in heaven, that had sent the vision, and its object was to reveal what shall be in the latter days.

The vision itself and its interpretation we must reserve for our next paper. Thus far we have had only the preparation for it, but such a preparation as manifests its great importance, and also marks out Daniel as a man greatly beloved of God, and destined to fill a high place among men, and to hold a still higher place in the things that concern God's kingdom upon earth.

… IV.

THE DREAM OF NEBUCHADNEZZAR.

(DANIEL ii. 31-47.)

WONDERFULLY had the telling of this dream been prepared for. The intense agitation of the king's mind, the sleepless night, the conviction that his dream portended events of no common importance, and nevertheless the complete oblivion of that which had so excited him: all this seems to have irritated Nebuchadnezzar till he could endure no delay, nor bear to wait till calmer moments brought back to his memory the visions that had disturbed his rest. He had tried resolutely again and again to recall and give shape to the vague images that still floated in his mind, but in vain; and the more he failed himself, the more determined he was that the wise men of his kingdom should unravel his enigma for him. For what reason did they enjoy wealth, rank, power, except because of their influence with the immortals? and they must now make good their claims. And when they would not even make the attempt, his rage knew no bounds, and he determined to massacre the whole of a class of men of great weight in the state, looked upon by the people almost with awe, and who had often ministered to his ambition, his glory, and his pleasures. Hitherto he had greatly honoured them; but Nebuchadnezzar was not a scrupulous nor a merciful man, and he was now in a state of frenzy. Woe to those who could not quiet the spirit and gratify the demand of an Oriental despot!

But when all his usual resources had failed him, the gratification of his demand came from an unexpected quarter. A handsome Jewish boy steps forward, and modestly disclaiming all personal merit, declares that his God will, for the king's sake, that he may know the things that shall come to pass, disclose to him the thoughts that had come into his mind upon his bed. Now the Jewish God was not like other gods. They were patient, much-enduring beings, who, as long as their own prerogatives were not interfered with, cared not how many rivals were admitted into their Pantheon. In the cuneiform inscriptions the worshipper delights in stringing together a long catalogue of the names of deities, who are pleased rather than offended at finding themselves forming part of so numerous an assembly. His fear is lest he should omit some one who would be angry at the neglect. Such a thought as that they would dispute one another's claims lay entirely outside the circle of his ideas. The God of the Jews was a "jealous" God. His prophets taught that these motley gods were nonentities, and that their worship, so impure and unholy in itself, was also an offence to true and real religion, because it gave to idols, the work of men's hands, the honour due to the One Almighty, who had made heaven and earth, and all things and beings that are therein.

Naturally this one exclusive God was the object of heathen dislike; and hence the pride of the king when he plundered the Temple of Jehovah at Jerusalem, and brought the holy vessels away in triumph to "the treasure-house of his own god." But now from this unlikely quarter came the allaying of his irritation. We know that in after-time the king often came in contact with the prophet Jeremiah, and learnt from him that he was Jehovah's chosen servant to make many nations drink of the cup of the Divine justice (Jer. xxv. 9). At present he knew of Jehovah only as a conquered Deity, and Daniel and his friends only as captive youths that were to minister to the pride and pomp of his court. He was soon to learn more true ideas of them both.

And when the dream was told him, how strange must his oblivion of it have seemed! It was so strongly marked, so extraordinary, and yet so natural, that he must have wondered how he could have forgotten it. Colossal statues, such as that which he himself set up in the plain of Dura, were common at Babylon. In his great buildings he must himself have erected many; but this one was remarkable, because it seemed as if the artist had attempted much more than he could accomplish. The conception was grand, the form masterly and awful; but, beginning with the most costly materials, the designer had ended with miry clay. An image so strangely composed ought to have impressed itself upon the king's memory. And its fate was as wonderful as was its fashion. A stone cut out without hands, self-originated and self-moving, strikes this mighty colossus. No visible force impels it; no human agency causes its activity. Yet it wars against the image, smites it, and grinds it to powder. Now there were no stones in Babylonia; all Nebuchadnezzar's buildings were of brick; for the soil of the country is alluvial, brought down from Armenia by the action of the rivers Tigris and Euphrates. The foreign stone therefore indicated external influence, but not human influence, nor one of a natural kind. It was something self-originating, and therefore must come from a being endowed with free-will. And as it was impelled by no human or natural power, the author of it must be Divine. And he saw that it went on calmly, quietly, and irresistibly till every other influence was crushed and broken, and itself as a mighty "mountain filled the whole earth."

Let us take, first, the general aspect of the image, and next its several parts.

VER. 31.—The image was of an excellent brightness and its form terrible. This is the aspect of earthly dominion. Surrounded by every form of majesty and splendour, it shines as with magic brilliancy; but this external beauty gilds and adorns the crushing strength of despotic power. This power may be used for good. It may give peace and security to the subject, and enable even the meanest to enjoy the fruit of his own toil. Too often in those old world-powers, built up by military skill, and resting upon no basis but force, the might of empire was used only to gratify the pride, the lust, and the caprice of the ruler. The subject had no legal rights; and even well-meaning men, who at the beginning of their reigns started well, soon found arbitrary power too strong for their virtues, and ended by becoming the scourge of their subjects. In spite, then, of its excellent brightness, the form thereof was terrible.

And yet one more reason for this terror. The empires symbolised in this image were not the native legitimate governments of races and peoples. They were the great military monarchies which endeavoured by force of arms to make the whole world as then known subject to them. Force was their weapon, and with it they crushed the rights and freedom of others. Hence the colossal size of the image; hence it was that it stood alone. These attempts at universal empire indirectly wrought some good. The conquests of Alexander carried with them trade and civilisation; those of Rome taught people the value of law. Even the Assyrian and Persian monarchies broke down barriers of -exclusiveness, and brought men into contact with one another, and so aided in the development and education of mankind. But the process involved a vast amount of human suffering; and if in this vision these empires seemed bright and majestic in the eyes of the Assyrian, to Daniel they appeared afterwards as cruel and ferocious wild beasts.

VERS. 32, 37, 38.—But let us consider the several parts of the image. The head was of gold. By this was symbolised the Babylonian monarchy, and virtually Nebuchadnezzar himself; for with him it began, and with him its vigour ended. There intervened only a short period of internal decay between his death and the allotted period of its duration. By the description of it as of "fine gold" is not meant that absolutely the Babylonian monarchy was good: but, first of all, the representation of the image is as it appeared to the king himself; and secondly, we are taught that each monarchy was inferior to the preceding. The Jewish prophets looked forward to better times. The Messiah was to bring them their golden age. Greek and Roman poets thought that the golden age had passed, and that each succeeding age would be worse and more unhappy than that which had gone before. Nebuchadnezzar shared in this heathen view, only he could conceive of no better age than his own. He, his empire, and his times were the world's era of gold; slowly but surely there would come decay and corruption. For gold there would be silver, and for silver would come brass, and for brass iron and clay. A true religion gives men hope; makes them look forward with confidence to the future; and because of that hope they labour to make things better. For the God whom they love and worship governs all things, and will order the course of events for man's real and final good. And when men in the present day bid us work for the regeneration of mankind, and tell us that we must try to raise the species, and so on, the belief in human improvement, and in the duty of labouring for it, are thoughts that have been learnt from the religion which they exhort us to discard. Their teaching would take away all motive for so labouring, and destroy the convictions upon which the belief in the possibility of human improvement rests. The victory that overcomes the world and the selfishness of our narrow hearts is not a vague theory about the perfectibility of the human race, but a belief in God's government of the world, and in His purposes of mercy and grace for the creatures whom He made, and whom now He invites to be the recipients of His love.

After magnifying the grandeur of Nebuchadnezzar's kingdom in terms appropriate to a universal monarchy, Daniel next describes the breast and arms of silver as being the symbol of an empire inferior to that of Babylon. The old commentators all consider this to have been a prophecy of the Medo-Persian empire, which succeeded the Babylonian. The new critics attempt diverse explanations, because they start with the assumption that there is no such thing as prophecy, and that what we assert to have been predictions were really the description of events written after they had taken place. Now as they cannot put the date of the book later than the reign of Antiochus Epiphanes, they have to find four empires prior to that period to which they may refer the symbols both here and in the prophecy of the four beasts (chap. vii.) Abiding by the old and perfectly satisfactory explanation, which alone gives a reasonable interpretation of the "stone cut out without hands," we have no doubt that this kingdom was that of the Medes and Persians, which was really one, though at its head were two nations represented by the two arms. It was not inferior in extent or duration, unless we consider that the first empire included the Ninevite as well as the Babylonian monarchies; and Cyrus was a far nobler character than Nebuchadnezzar. But it sank into effeminacy, and perished from the feebleness that resulted from the general decay caused by the immorality of its court.

The third kingdom is of brass, but it " bears rule over all the earth." Brass or bronze, an alloy of copper and tin, was the metal used for weapons, and the Greeks were not merely brave soldiers, but were thoroughly well armed. Countries unknown to the Babylonians were conquered by Alexander; and

Greece, which had stood the shock of the invading hosts of Persia, acknowledged his sway. And so far from being inferior to Babylon, Greece was in every way the nobler power, and the Macedonian conquests were the cause of infinite good. But the founder's life was cut short by intemperance, and his empire was broken into fragments before it had even been consolidated into an orderly whole.

"The fourth kingdom is strong as iron," strong chiefly to break in pieces and subdue. For many centuries Rome was ever fighting and winning battles. It was at first but a single town of no great size, but war was its pastime and its trade. Irresistible in the battlefield, within there was internal weakness, the struggle of fierce factions, civil dissensions, and finally an oligarchy of rich men, before whom all manliness vanished away, and Italy became the property of a class who cultivated it by gangs of slaves. To save itself it had to bow to the yoke of absolute power, and at length, from the necessities of administration, was divided into the Western and Eastern empires, symbolised by the two legs, in which there was still vast strength, but also much weakness, the extremities of the Roman dominions being constantly harassed by incursions of the barbarians, who often even carried their raids into the very heart of the empire. It was thus "partly strong and partly brittle" (see margin), because, while its armies of mercenaries were irresistible, its own subjects were too feeble to defend themselves; and its toes were of iron if protected by fortresses and regular armies, but of clay if these aids were withdrawn. As, finally, the government of this vast realm was ever the prize of revolt, of artifice, and of crime, the emperors were always trying to strengthen themselves by "mingling with the seed of men," by marriages with members of rival families; but in vain. Ambition was not quenched thereby, and many an intermarriage meant for peace only widened the hostile breach.

The dream carries the description of the Roman empire down to a period long subsequent to the founding of the Messiah's kingdom; and the ten toes may be identical with the ten horns of chap. vii. 7. And of Messiah's kingdom itself we have not merely the beginning, but the growth, until it had crushed and taken the place of all these empires. For it is important to observe that this is a vision of universal empires; and while the four which form the image all fail, the last becomes "a great mountain, and fills the whole earth," and "shall stand for ever."

THE DREAM OF NEBUCHADNEZZAR.

VERS. 33, 44.—This fifth monarchy is not of human origin. It is a "stone cut out without hands," which Daniel explains as meaning that "the God of heaven shall set up a kingdom." Some great battle or series of battles had established the empires of this world, subject of course to God's general providence, but making them seem to man the direct result of human effort.

God's empire is set up by One who did "not strive, nor cry, nor was His voice heard in the streets" (Matt. xii. 19). No conquering armies carried the creed of Jesus of Nazareth on to victory, as the Arabs won disciples for their prophet by the sword. It wrought and still works silently, by persuasion, by reaching the conscience of the individual, by speaking to the sad, the contrite, and the humble with a still small voice. So it wrought in that strong empire of resistless Rome. Its victories were noiseless, unsung by poets, celebrated by no triumphal arches or processions; and while the rulers were thinking of Christianity as the superstition of a feeble and powerless sect, to be extirpated by one imperial decree, it was filling their armies, their market-places, their fleets, their palaces, the work-houses of their slaves. Christians were everywhere; every place was full of them, and heathenism crumbled to pieces, ground to dust before an unseen

E

power. Twelve fishermen, without military skill, or human influence, or eloquence, or learning, set up a kingdom which strives after universal dominion and has the promise of ultimate success.

It was from Mount Zion that this stone was launched (Isa. ii. 3); for upon it there died a meek and lowly sufferer, condemned by human injustice to a malefactor's death. But that malefactor is the king of a world-wide empire. A crown of thorns girt His brow: before that crown all the emblems of earthly sovereignty have bowed down, and the cross on which that sufferer died has been elevated to be the symbol which holds the topmost place in the diadems of the chief earthly monarchs of mankind. A rude soldiery arrayed Him in robes of purple. Never has monarch reigned clad in more royal glory than the calm and patient victim of those rough mercenaries. Eighteen centuries and more have passed away, but no throne is so secure as the throne of Jesus; for He reigns in the willing hearts of His people, and they have a warm devotion and a loving allegiance to Him which would make them, were troubled times to arise, as ready now for the pains of martyrdom as were the faithful of old. For "His kingdom shall never be destroyed, nor shall it be left to other people." The Persians robbed Assyria of the sceptre, the Greeks tore it from the Persians, the Romans from the Greeks. Christ is an eternal King, and His people will have none to take their place; for the very gates of hell will be powerless against the kingdom of our God and of His Christ.

And it has still battles to fight—spiritual battles, and victories to win, but victories of peace and love. For though the faith of Christ has grown into a mountain, it does not yet fill all the earth. And of this the reason is, that though the stone is cut out without hands, yet God has deigned to associate man with Him in the task of establishing the empire of His dear Son. Not because such human aid is necessary, but because man attains to the purpose of his own existence and is ennobled by being a fellow-worker with God. He who gains a victory for Christ fulfils thereby the object for which he was born into this world. We are placed here in the midst of trouble and sorrow, of temptation and sin, of struggle and effort, in order that we may through these very trials win our heavenward way to joy and perfectness; and amid all our difficulties we are supported by the conviction that the sufferings of this present time are not worthy to be compared with the glory that shall be revealed hereafter. In earnestly endeavouring, therefore, to win the world for Christ, to alleviate its pains, redress its wrongs, obtain for it purity, peace, love, holiness, we are also fulfilling the Divine purpose for which God constituted this world such as it is, and placed us here upon it.

And thus, then, the captive Jewish youth unrolled before the eyes of the tyrant that had crushed his country, his home, and the temple of his God, the course of the five universal empires. Four rise one after another, each to fall. For a while they beat down and destroy, and fill the fair surface of the earth with tears and misery; for their weapons are force, violence, and cruelty; and scarcely has one seized the sceptre before another rises to wrench it from his loosening grasp. At length, ushered in by no trumpet-blast, with no clashing of arms nor banners fluttering in the breeze, but by a still, calm, unseen influence, the fifth empire begins to arise. Its armies are recruited from the poor, the outcast, the slave. Those whom men despise are summoned to its standard; and that standard is one of suffering. It is a cross, telling of shame and of a malefactor's death. But "with this for thy symbol thou shalt conquer." It has its heroes; they are martyrs, who bear the utmost cruelty that debased man can invent, and bear it with joy, for their love of Him who gave His life for them. It has its warriors—men who give up all worldly pleasures, and honours, and gain that they may carry far and wide the good tidings of there being salvation for mankind. It has its armies—myriads whose joy it is to do good and bear evil for their Master's sake. And the regeneration of mankind will come when this host, struggling for love, and purity, and holiness, has won the world for its Lord.

It was but a dim outline that Daniel unfolded before the king. In long vista he saw empire succeeding empire, until one arose that would stand for ever. And the king knew that his dream had been such as the youthful seer before him had declared; he felt, too, that its meaning had been rightly interpreted; and, awe-struck, "he fell upon his face and worshipped Daniel, and commanded that they should offer an oblation and sweet odours unto him." Daniel was to him the interpreter of the God of heaven, and as such seemed to him to be Divine. We may be sure that Daniel would allow of no idolatrous adoration, and the words of the next verse show that he quickly led the king's mind into a more true channel. For "the king answered unto Daniel, and said, Of a truth it is, that your God is a God of gods, and a Lord of kings, and a revealer of secrets."

V.

A CONSTRAINED CONFESSION.

(DANIEL ii. 46–49.)

IN our previous chapter we have seen the king's mind so agitated by the troubled thoughts which followed upon his dream, that, losing all self-control, he ordered the wise men, who had failed to satisfy an unreasonable command, to be put to death and their colleges razed to the ground. And by this we can measure his feelings as he listened to the youthful stripling before him, first recalling to his memory the strange images which had flitted before his mind in his broken slumbers, and then explaining to him their meaning. It was a mighty panorama, unfolding the course of the world's history, revealing to him a succession of claimants for universal empire, and finally asserting that God would set up a kingdom for Himself, which would extend over all lands, and rule them with a sceptre which time should never weaken nor external force destroy. Secure from outward violence and internal decay, it would break in pieces all earthly kingdoms and itself stand for ever.

Now if it was gratifying to Nebuchadnezzar to know that he was the head of gold, there was also humiliation in the announcement that his empire was so soon to pass away, and that it was merely one of several empires which were in succession to prepare the way for a kingdom which was not to be of human founding. And it is a lesson equally unwelcome to rulers now. The stone cut out without hands has become a mighty power, ruling over the hearts and consciences of men. Side by side with it stand the empires of this world, wielding all earthly authority, with armies and fleets at their disposal, and invested with that majesty and splendour which made "the brightness of this image excellent, and the form thereof terrible." Now we believe that these earthly empires all have their work to do for Christ; and that they have it assigned to them under the same condition of free will counterbalanced by responsibility, which regulates all human working. If they do their work for Christ He will acknowledge them, and give them strength and continuance. If they refuse, then must they give place to others. Of Churches we are expressly taught that Christ walks among the golden candlesticks to see and judge and reward and punish; and that a Church which does not labour for Him will have its candlestick removed out of its place (Rev. ii. 1, 5). We learn the same truth here of earthly kingdoms. They have each their place and order and duty; but their time and duration and greatness depend upon their work for God.

And God rules over and among them, but so, nevertheless, as to have made it a universal law that His work has to be done by man. The stone is indeed " cut out without hands ; " for the gospel is no human scheme, nor was it founded for human ends, by man's device, or craft, or forethought. Like its Founder, Christ's kingdom is a plant that has grown out of a dry ground, where earthly vegetation there was none. But as its purpose is to raise and ennoble man, very much is left to man. It aids, assists, encourages, strengthens him, but it does not dispense with him. It summons him to work, enables him by Divine help to do that which is far above his natural powers, and by noble service it elevates, perfects, and blesses him. And the man who has made his heart the temple of the Holy Ghost is by His indwelling rendered fit for the higher service which doubtless awaits the redeemed in heaven.

But we must not so interpret the doctrine of God's overruling providence as to suppose that His work on earth goes on just the same whether man obey or whether he resist. Doubtless at the last day we shall find that God has done all things well; and that His work has moved onward steadily, "breaking to pieces the iron, the clay, the brass, the silver, and the gold, and making all alike as the chaff of the summer threshing-floors; but this is so when we look down upon earth as God looks down upon it from the height of His Divine majesty. It is not so when we look at earthly things through the medium of human thought, and from our own level. Then we see God's work delayed, from the absence in Churches of missionary effort. We see religion declining from want of earnestness in its professors. We see kingdoms falling from their high place, and crumbling in long decay, because rulers and people have not recognised their duty to God, and done the work to which He called them. And other kingdoms and Churches we see rising in power and prospering because they are earnestly trying to labour for God, and to spend and be spent for Him.

Looked at in its true light, it is a great privilege for man thus to be made a fellow-worker with God. And the delay, and even the apparent frustration of the Divine purpose is permitted, because the present constitution of things is for man's good and upward progress. God, the all-perfect, needs not this chequered earthly state of things for His own happiness : it is a purpose of benevolence and love intended for man's restoration. Thus man is left free, because only in a state of freedom can He render to God true service and do His will. And by serving God and bowing his human will to the Divine good pleasure he attains to a regenerate life and to a fitness for the perfect service and diviner life to be enjoyed in God's presence.

Now as Nebuchadnezzar listened to Daniel, and heard for the first time of the existence upon earth of a kingdom of the God of heaven, and saw unfolded before him this map of empires rising and falling, but all alike preparing for a kingdom that should never fall, awe took possession of his heart, and the youthful seer seemed to him, not as some magician or astrologer that had rightly read the message of the stars, but as one moved by the Spirit of God ; and falling down before him, he recognised him in his true greatness as the representative of the Deity. Nebuchadnezzar knew as yet but little of God. This was the first of the many lessons vouchsafed to him. It roused up new perceptions, gave him fresh ideas; but at the end of it he had only advanced a very little way in his knowledge of heavenly things. For Daniel's God was to him still only one of many gods; but at least he felt that He was a very real and true God, and that Daniel had been His spokesman.

We read, therefore (ver. 46), "Then the king Nebuchadnezzar fell upon his face, and worshipped Daniel, and commanded that they should offer an oblation and sweet odours unto him." Now when the people of Lystra wished to offer sacrifice to Paul and Barnabas, because of the great miracle that they had wrought, the apostles were shocked beyond measure, and indignantly rejected the bestowal on them of that homage which belonged to God only. Here Daniel accepted the sweet odours and oblation. Whence came conduct apparently so different? But, first, the people of Lystra supposed that their false gods had assumed human form; and they would therefore have been confirmed in their heathenish superstition had Paul and Barnabas accepted the proffered sacrifice. Here the honour is done to the true God, and Nebuchadnezzar was rising above the level of his old creed, though he had not yet attained to the full light of truth. And next, the sacrifice at Lystra was to be offered absolutely to Paul and Barnabas as themselves Divine beings. Now Nebuchadnezzar made no such mistake. His view was that "the Spirit of the Holy Gods" rested upon Daniel; and in the words which he spake he clearly distinguished between Daniel and Daniel's God. And therefore Daniel did not reject an honour which he probably felt to be excessive and even superstitious. The king was on the right road to truth, and he did nothing to call away his attention from the main point to that which was of lesser value.

The word *worshipped* means indeed no more than that the king prostrated himself before Daniel. But this was an extraordinary act. For Nebuchadnezzar was an absolute monarch, a despot, who by his military skill and genius for government had made himself the most powerful sovereign of his time; and the man before whom he thus bowed to the ground was a youth, a captive, with no earthly power or greatness. Nor was he content with prostrating himself before him, but commanded that an oblation—an offering, that is, of food and wine—should be made to him, and incense burnt before him. But though there was excess and somewhat of heathenish superstition in the command, yet Nebuchadnezzar did not confound Daniel with God. He had spoken too plainly of the God of heaven for such confusion to be possible, and Daniel was thus honoured because that heavenly Deity had spoken by his mouth.

This plainly appears from the words that follow; for Nebuchadnezzar says, "Of a truth it is that your God is a God of gods, and a Lord of kings, and a revealer of secrets, seeing thou couldst reveal this secret."

Now sometimes, as in chap. xi. 36, this title "God of gods" means the only true God. God's own people meant by it that Jehovah was the one sole and only Deity among all those who arrogated to themselves this title. But Nebuchadnezzar meant far less. Natural as seems to us the doctrine of their being only one God, it was not so with the heathen. Their deities were beings but little higher than themselves; and thus their fancy filled earth and air and sea with a motley variety of gods and demigods, whose powers and attributes often clashed one with another. They had not, and could not grasp, that belief which is the great comfort and joy of the Christian, that one Supreme Being fills all things with His presence, governs all things by His almighty will, and guides all things by His omniscient wisdom. No such grand central truth gave stability to the life of a heathen; no such conviction comforted him under the changing aspect of his earthly fortunes and sustained him in trial and sorrow. Yet what Nebuchadnezzar acknowledged was something far in advance of his former tenets. For not only did he confess that the God of this captive Jew was mightier than his own deities, but he declared that He was supreme. For "God of gods" meant that He was over all others, and that they must obey Him. His own idols still seemed to him to be real powers, but subordinate; he did not disbelieve in Bel and Nebo, but he felt that there was a God above and beyond them, whom they must serve. As he was himself "king of kings," one as high above other kings as they were above their subjects, so was Daniel's God as high above other gods as they were high above men.

It was Nebuchadnezzar's first lesson, valuable, but not perfect; an introduction to truth, but not the full truth itself. And even the heathen sometimes ascended thus high by the mere light of reason. We find the Greeks often acknowledging that behind and above the deities whom the people worshipped there must be some controlling power which even the gods must obey. In this, as in much besides, they were groping in the dark after truth; and as truth was what they sought, God granted them some measure of it. But the Bible at its very beginning rises to truth more perfect, more complete, more satisfying to heart and mind than the best conclusions of Greek wisdom; for it tells us of one God, the sole Creator of the universe, who by His word made all things, and from whom all things in heaven and in earth have their being and proceed.

The truth to which Nebuchadnezzar had attained was far less than this; for he did not as yet see God as the one sole power who had called all other things into existence for His own glory. But it led to practical results; for he also acknowledged that Daniel's God was a "Lord of kings," one to whom kings were responsible, and whom they must obey. His views probably were confused and indistinct; nor was he one who would let any sense of his obligations to an unseen power interfere with his own despotic will. But it was this sense, probably, of his responsibility to Daniel's God which made him so honour the prophet; and as thus the oblation and incense were rightly meant, they were not rejected.

Two points still remain: the first, Daniel's elevation to power; the second, his affection for his friends.

Just as twelve centuries before Pharaoh had raised Joseph to power because he had revealed to him the secret of his dreams, so was it at Babylon with Daniel. Now the heroes of the world rise to eminence and authority by earthly qualities. It is by eloquence, or military skill, or some startling piece of statesmanship that they leave their obscurity and attain to splendour; too often even by flattering the vanity or by gratifying the caprice or the passion of some monarch or of the populace. The heroes of the Bible rise by God's blessing, and generally by its being made manifest that they are near to God and possess His favour and protection. It was his saintliness which commended Daniel to Nebuchadnezzar, and he made him ruler, first of all, over the city of Babylon and the country in its immediate neighbourhood; and, secondly, he appointed him to be chief over those colleges of wise men, by whom he had just been trained, and among whom before he had held so humble a position.

And here we recognise the hand of God's providence clearly revealed. Just as in Egypt the family of Jacob were to be formed into a nation, and Joseph was raised to power and high dignity that he might protect them; so at Babylon they were to be reformed, and made fit to be Christ's apostles and missionaries at His coming, and Daniel was made governor that he might be their friend and comforter. We read of God's high purpose in sending them into exile in Jer. xxiv. 5, 6, xxix. 10-14. What a blessing must Daniel have been to them! How greatly must he have lightened the heavy burden of their captivity! And how powerfully must his example have strengthened their faith, and encouraged them to love and serve their God! To Daniel must have been largely due that fervent piety and ardent patriotism which shone so brightly in Ezra and Nehemiah and the returning Jews.

Lastly, in his hour of elevation Daniel did not forget his three friends. He had joined them with him in his prayers (ver. 17); together had their petitions mounted up to God; and now the first petition which he offers to the king is that they may be associated with him in the responsibilities of his office. It was granted, and he had the happiness of feeling that those whose duty it would be to carry out his orders were dear friends whom he could trust. For himself there was even higher rank; for he "sat in the gate of the king;" in other words, he was his confidential adviser and chief minister, whose duty it was to be in constant attendance upon the sovereign.

At the opening of the book we saw Daniel and his three friends in the depth of their misery. Torn from their homes, and separated from those whom they held most dear, they had been condemned to slavery and galling service under a despotic king. Selected next for special training in a kind of learning that must often have grated upon their consciences, they gave evidence of an earnest self-denying faith, and by God's blessing were rescued from contamination. But scarcely was their training complete before the decree went forth that they must be put to death, because their masters had failed to declare a dream which the king had himself forgotten; and again their faith gained the victory. In answer to their prayers God revealed to them the secret, and now they are raised to a position of great power and usefulness; but one wherein they must again be tried, to the end that their faith, perfected by victory, may enable them to be foremost in the great work of regenerating at Babylon God's preparatory Church. It was their grand office to summon the Jews back to renewed earnestness and fresh and vigorous life, in place of the long decay, and faithlessness, and immorality which, in spite of the reforms of Hezekiah and Josiah, had made them unworthy to bear witness for God during the last two centuries of their existence in the promised land. The Jewish Church had fallen, and must needs be brought back to a better life. Chastisement and exile alone would not have availed to work the change; it was wrought by the piety and zeal of Jeremiah at home, and of Daniel and his friends in the land of their captivity.

VI.

THE DURA IMAGE.

(DANIEL iii. 1–7.)

ST. JAMES tells us that "the rich should rejoice in that he is made low," and God mercifully sent Daniel and his friends such trial as was necessary for their spiritual advancement. They had enjoyed temporal success and exaltation. Daniel had entered the king's presence as a captive lad, who had been selected to study the language and learning of his conquerors, not from any feeling of kindness to himself, but that he might be trained to stand among the numerous slaves who ministered to the pride and pomp of an Oriental despot. He had entered there, too, under sentence of death, but he had displayed such wisdom, such extraordinary skill in interpreting the king's dream, such modest courage and fortitude and truthfulness, that the king had recognised in him something more than mere human gifts, and had therefore made obeisance to him, had treated him as a demi-god, and had even made him ruler of the home province of Babylon, and at his request had given high place to his three friends in the government under him.

An advance so rapid might have led to moral declension on the part of these young men. Already their lives had been most eventful, and the piety that had grown in the shade might have withered in the sunshine of prosperity. In mercy, therefore, to them, and for the good of the Jewish exiles, there was still a terrible trial for them to undergo; and their faith again won the victory, and thereby became so strong and massive that henceforth no storm could overthrow them from their firm foundations. And with them the whole nation grew strong, and learned to trust in the Lord God of their fathers.

Their trial came in this wise: "Nebuchadnezzar the king made an image of gold." We have seen even in his treatment of Daniel that he was still an untutored heathen; for he paid him something like Divine honours, and while acknowledging Daniel's God as a "God of gods," he was very far from knowing that there is and can be but one sole God. We find in the cuneiform inscriptions mention of a whole pantheon of gods and goddesses worshipped in Chaldea. Among these Nebuchadnezzar had doubtless some patron deity. It may have been Nebo; for his own name means "Nebo protects from trouble." His father, Nabopolassar, also bore a name compounded with that of the same deity; and as Nebuchadnezzar rebuilt his temple at Borsippa, and also dedicated to him the seaport which he formed on the Persian Gulf, we may conclude that he was the king's tutelary god. His name is the same as the Hebrew word Nabi, *prophet*, and he was regarded as the god of knowledge and eloquence, of learning and literature. They represented him, further, as the eldest son of Ishtar, the planet Venus as the evening star, herself the daughter of the moon-god. All these absurdities never grated upon the reason of the Babylonian wise men; possibly they never seriously reflected upon them. For after all, their gods were not spiritual beings, who loved truth and holiness; they were but the powerful, pleasure-loving, capricious inhabitants of another sphere, capable of doing endless mischief, delighted to receive honour from their worshippers, vindictive if it were withheld. Polytheism is a thing most degrading to men morally and mentally; and probably Nebuchadnezzar's view of his tutelary god was that he was a powerful servitor, bound to make him a handsome recompense for his worship of him, but one who would never trouble himself

THE DURA IMAGE.

about such things as the cruelty which was so marked a characteristic of the king's conduct.

In honour, then, of this deity Nebuchadnezzar set up a colossal statue, shaped in the form of a man—for so the Hebrew word signifies—of gold, but not necessarily solid. The word more probably means that it was overlaid with gold: and it was perhaps raised upon a pedestal of some baser material, as the reason of its vast size seems to have been to make it visible throughout the whole plain of Dura at sunrise, the hour of prayer. We read in the "Speaker's Com." on this passage that "during the trigonometrical survey of Mesopotamia, Captain Selby ascertained that in the level plain of Dura the dip of the horizon at twelve miles is fifty-three feet." Now this image was sixty cubits, that is, seventy-five feet, in height, and seven and a half feet in breadth. When then the sun struck upon the shining metal in the morning it would be visible all round Babylon to a distance of from fifteen to twenty miles. We are not told the date at which these occurrences took place, but it is reasonable to suppose that it was soon after the conquest of Egypt. Nebuchadnezzar would see there the colossal statues erected near the lake Moeris in honour of the kings of the twelfth dynasty, represented each in a sitting posture, and placed every one upon the summit of its own pyramid. It was probably the sight of these vast figures, visible in level Egypt to a great distance, which suggested the idea to the Babylonian king; and the statue was probably a memorial and thank-offering for the success which in Egypt and elsewhere had crowned his arms, and was made of the gold which he had plundered from the Egyptian temples. He had probably long ago forgotten the interview between himself and Daniel, and was elated and made haughty and self-confident by a long career of victory.

There had probably been long preparation for the eventful day. The army of veteran warriors had returned and paraded the country, displaying their spoils. The king at its head had been received with humble prostrations, and all that self-abasement and degradation with which an Oriental bows before the representative, not of law and righteousness, but of force. The most famous artists had been gathered to decide upon the attitude and features of the god, the size and shape had been carefully modelled, the plates of gold skilfully laid over the frame, and at last all was ready for the feast of dedication. And so finally the command goes forth that all the great officials of the realm shall gather round the king for the setting up of the image.

THE DURA IMAGE.

This gathering of the chiefs would take some months; for messengers, runners on foot, would be sent out, with proper credentials and commands to the governors to forward them with all speed upon their way; and when the royal despatches had been received, each noble would make his preparations according to his rank, and would at last start on his journey with a numerous retinue, all taking with them tents and everything they would need upon their travels. The list of officials gives us a high idea, not only of the pomp of Nebuchadnezzar's court, but also of the efficiency of his government. Those first mentioned are the " 'Chashdarfana," whence our word "satrap," shortened from "chashdraf." They were the governors of provinces, where they reigned in well-nigh regal splendour. We read of them also in Esther iii. 12, where they are called in our version "the king's lieutenants," which is a more correct rendering than "princes," because their dignity was solely derived from the king's appointment, and not from birth or hereditary right. Next to the satraps came the Sagans, translated "governors" here and in chap. ii. 48. They were the lieutenants of the satraps, just as the satraps were the king's vicegerents. In chap. ii. 48 they are similarly those next in rank to the chief ruler, but not, as here, in military matters, but in the college of the wise men. Next come the Pachwata, or pashas, inferior governors; and next the Adar-gazraya. *Adar* means chief, and is used like our word " arch ;" while *gazer* was the title of some class of wise men (see chap. ii. 27; iv. 7). Interpreted by the help of these passages it probably means " chief soothsayers," who would be the archbishops of the Chaldean realm. The Gedabraya, who came next, were treasurers who had charge of the revenues of the various satrapies. The Detabraya, or counsellors, were the jurisprudents, men who interpreted the law, and would answer to our judges. The Tiftaya, the root of which word appears in Mufti, were probably inferior judges, but as the word occurs only here, its meaning is uncertain. Finally, all the rulers of each province, all the officials of the various districts, were to accompany their chiefs.

And having thus provided for a large and glorious concourse of high nobles at this grand ceremony in honour of so many victories, and of the establishment of so vast an empire, as they stood marshalled in order, according to their rank, a herald made proclamation as follows :—

" To you it is commanded, O people, nations, and languages," &c.

Now God has probably appointed a diversity of languages to be a means for breaking up mankind into separate nations. In the eleventh chapter of Genesis we find that the effect of all men using one tongue was the fostering of human arrogance; and the very purpose of the tower of Babel appears to have been the establishment and maintenance of a universal monarchy. When on the day of Pentecost the universal kingdom of our Lord was set up on earth, this confusion of tongues was for the time healed by a miracle, in token that in God's realm of love there should be but one language. And towards this noble consummation things seem now to be tending; for every year the number of those who speak the English tongue is increasing in large excess of those who speak any other language, and the central bond of those who thus speak our language is undoubtedly the English Bible. If the increase of the English-speaking race proceeds in the same proportion during the next half century as has prevailed during the last fifty years, it will not only be foremost, as it is already in power and influence, but it will be absolutely the largest in respect of actual numbers. And we may even venture to say that the reason why God has given to this race its rapid increase, its dominance in both hemispheres, and its vast influence, is because God has appointed it to be His instrument for the setting up throughout the world of that universal monarchy "which shall never be destroyed, and of which the rule shall not be left to another people." Already England and America are foremost in missionary effort, and in the printing and circulation of the Word of God. But as yet it is but a feeble effort, and when the whole English-speaking population awakens to a sense of its greatness, and of the high purpose for which God has bestowed upon it so large an extension and so high a place, the kingdoms of the earth will rapidly be made the kingdoms of our God, and upon the ground, now being with so great toil prepared for it, will rise "the great mountain which shall fill all the earth."

Nebuchadnezzar's universal empire, with its pompous address to the "peoples, nations, and languages," was but a poor counterfeit of God's universal empire; but it is a fact worth reflecting upon, that man is ever attempting to compass in some way of his own that which God also purposes to accomplish in His perfect way. God has given to Christ the kingdoms of this world, and of His dominion there shall be no end, and He shall reign for ever and ever. But it is a kingdom of love and truth, which by the weapons of persuasion shall gain its victories to bless and comfort and ennoble all who are vanquished by it. But man is made in God's image, after His likeness, and many of the noblest minds have dreamed of a universal empire to be set up by force of arms, and maintained by mechanical and intellectual supremacy. This would not really be for man's good; nay, it would work only for evil. As it is, each language has its own peculiarities, which are at once the result and perpetuating cause of a varied mental development. What a loss it would have been to the world if the Greek or the Latin language had never existed! How greatly are our minds enriched by the masterpieces produced in the many languages of modern Europe! And so in science and art and commerce each portion of mankind has its special gifts, and works for the common good. Nor is the contribution of each kingdom in proportion to its size or population. The greater effort required to maintain their well-being often calls forth higher qualities in the inhabitants of some nation whose political importance is but small. No greater misfortune could happen to mankind than for one kingdom to dominate over the rest. Often has the attempt been made, but always the providence of God has brought it to nought. And in His own universal empire the common bond will be a common faith, and the worship of the same Father in heaven, and of Jesus Christ our Lord. But it will not crush out the rights of peoples or of individuals, and the nations without distrust or fear will all of them keep " the bounds of their habitation determined for them" (Acts xvii. 26).

The musical instruments mentioned in the fifth verse have led to much controversy, it having been asserted that they are mostly of Greek origin; and from this assumption the conclusion has been inferred that the Book of Daniel was written in the time of the Maccabees, when the Greek language had been made dominant by the conquests of Alexander. But modern investigations have shown that Greek trade with the continent of Asia is of vast antiquity. Caravans carried Greek goods far and wide, and their native names went with them. No philologer is now surprised at finding the Greek name for a knife in a document so old as the last words of Jacob; nor at translating, "instruments of cruelty are their knives" (Gen. xlix. 5). The pastoral tribes of Palestine knew nothing about metallurgy, and their cutting instruments were all imported from Greece. Those of Jacob's sons were probably knives of bronze.

But the assertion that the names of these instruments are Greek is a rash one. The names of the horn and of the flute—literally *whistler*, and probably, therefore, some sort of pipe—are confessedly Semitic. The harp is literally the *cither*, or guitar, probably the oldest musical instrument in the world. The usual Hebrew and Syriac name is *chinnor*, which also found its way as *kinur* into the Greek language. Alike in ancient and modern times the name is most widely spread, being found in almost every tongue, and it is formed, as our ears tell us, from the sound made by the vibration of the strings. But though found in Greek, it is not a Greek word, but belongs to some primeval tongue. The next instrument has been translated " sackbut," not from any idea that this was the true meaning of the word, but because there is a similarity of sound between the two names. The sackbut is a sort of bagpipe, while the *sabcha* was a stringed instrument of a triangular shape, producing sounds so sharp as to be disagreeable. It also found its way into Greece and Rome, carrying its Oriental name with it, slightly altered into *sambuca*. The next instrument is the psanterin, which looks like the Greek word *psalterion*, but there are many difficulties, as Dr. Pusey pointed out in his " Lectures on Daniel," in this identification.

There is nothing, however, surprising in Greek

musical instruments being found at such an emporium of commerce as Babylon, and at the court of a great king. But when we come to the last name, "symphonia," translated *dulcimer*, we are compelled to hesitate at the conclusion that any of these words are really Greek. For here we have undoubtedly a Greek word, while the thing is as certainly Oriental. We have, in fact, here an illustration of the well-known principle that people always endeavour to give a meaning to foreign words admitted into their language. Thus the French *chaussée* is altered by us into "causeway," because it thus seems to become intelligible to those who only understand their native tongue. The instrument itself is the Oriental sephonya, called by the Italians *zampogna*, and in old French *chifonie*. It seems to have been a sort of reed-pipe, and the Greek word "symphony," that is, "unison of sound," gave no better idea of the instrument than "causeway" does of the French *chaussée*. Meier derives the word from a root signifying *to draw together*, as if it too was a kind of bagpipe; but really the names of musical instruments are some of the oldest of all existent words, and their general prevalence is one of the many arguments in proof of a common origin for languages finally so remote as the Semitic and the Aryan families of tongues.

But though thus proclaimed to the sound of sweet music, it was a stern command that went forth. Nebuchadnezzar would allow no doubt or uncertainty as regards the homage to be paid to his god. As harp and horn and flute breathed forth their notes, all that vast assemblage of men, of the highest rank and famous for learning, were to throw themselves prostrate on the ground and offer worship. There were men there professing every form of belief: fire-worshippers who regarded all idols with abomination; men who worshipped two opposing principles, one good, one evil; others who had their own national gods, and who hated the gods of their conquerors as beings that had wronged them. It did not matter. In an empire of force, no man has any rights, and were any one daring enough to think and act for himself, his fate would be to "be cast that same hour into the midst of a burning fiery furnace."

What strange resistance was offered to the royal mandate we shall soon see, and we shall find that a true religion alone claims for its followers, and concedes even to those who reject it, freedom for the conscience. False religions and infidelity conspire in suppressing the rights of conscience. The infidel would crush religion by main force ; a false religion will allow no questioning of its creed. A true religion is a religion of love to others, and of holy boldness on the part of those who profess it. Its weapons are " love, joy, peace, long-suffering, kindness, goodness, faithfulness, meekness." But gentle though it be, it is strong to bear and suffer ; and no heroes have been so firm and steadfast as the martyrs of the Jewish and the Christian Church.

VII.

THE ACCUSATION.

(DANIEL iii. 8-15.)

WE have seen that the setting up of the colossal image in the plain of Dura was really an act of self-glorification. Nebuchadnezzar had no purpose of thanking God for his victories. It is one of the many beneficent results of Christianity that it humbles the victor in the hour of his pride. That great conquering race of old, the Romans, felt the necessity of this. Many a brave soldier probably had come home so elated by success, and hardened by the possession of absolute power, that his fellow-citizens could ill endure him. On the solemn day, therefore, when he entered their city in triumph, they placed behind him on the car on which he rode a slave, whose business it was to bend forward from time to time and whisper in his ear, "Look behind thee; remember that thou too art a man." Christianity acts in a far different way. It bids the victor look upward to God, and see in Him the giver of all good gifts; and thus it reminds him that it is God who has given him the victory, and that he is God's minister, and must use all he has and is for God's glory.

Now the prophet Jeremiah tells us (chap. xxv. 9) that Nebuchadnezzar was in an especial sense Jehovah's minister, raised up to perform certain definite duties. But the king thought that his great success, the wonderful victories that he had gained, and the vast empire which he had welded together by force of arms, were all the result of his own bravery, and skill, and vigour. And so on his return from Egypt he celebrated his conquests by setting up this image, and gathering together all the magnates of his realm to participate in the pomp of its dedication. Nominally he dedicated the image to Nebo; but Nebo was nothing more than the deity whose business it was to take care of him, and see that his wishes were accomplished. In the Babylonian inscriptions there is a great show of respect for a crowd of deities. They are all mentioned in due order, with flattering words of courtesy, and the respectful invocation of their aid. Most careful were even kings to do them all honour, because they were very capricious and easily offended and revengeful. But there was no submission to them of the will; no recognition

THE ACCUSATION. 101

in them of anything better or holier than human qualities; no obedience to them as the givers of law. They were powerful, mischievous, changeable; and so they must be kept in good-humour. There was no acknowledgment on the part of the heathen that God was just, and good, and true; and the favour of the Deity was, they supposed, to be won by the costliness of the gift, and not by the holy life of the worshipper.

And at length the day of Nebuchadnezzar's triumph had arrived. Marshalled upon a vast plain which extended itself in unbroken sameness to the verge of the horizon, stood all the pomp and strength and prowess of the Babylonian empire. The hour was probably the early morning. When the first rays of the rising sun lit up the head of the golden image, and made it visible far and wide, the music was to sound, and the whole concourse was to prostrate itself upon the ground. It would be a wonderful sight, such as no one present could ever forget. There is little twilight in those latitudes, and the transition from the deep dark blue of the sky, illumined by constellations which shine with brilliancy far exceeding that of the stars in our northern regions, to the splendour of a tropical day is rapid in the extreme. And as the sun shone forth, this colossus of gold would break upon the sight in dazzling radiance, and it would seem as if some god had indeed come down to earth.

But, as we have said, this concourse was not intended to do God honour. The thought of living and dying for God's glory is Christian, and not heathen. Even Judaism fell short of this elevation of thought, and only the religion of Christ teaches us without thought of self to refer all to God. If the Bible opens with the grand truth that one God created all things, it is in the last book of the New Testament that the words are added "And for thy pleasure they are and were created" (Rev. iv. 11).

Now heathenism attained to neither of these ennobling truths. It knew of no Creator, and understood, therefore, nothing of the relation which exists between man as God's workmanship and God as the maker, the owner, the preserver of the things He had created for His glory. The heathen had no idea of any relationship between him and his god, except that he was his patron and could help him occasionally, and always do him a great deal of harm. He had to treat him, therefore, with a great deal of deference and much show of outward respect. But it was not the honour of his god that was the first thought with

Nebuchadnezzar in summoning this vast gathering. It was pride in himself, elation at his victories, boastfulness and arrogance, that made him dedicate this mighty image, and summon all his chieftains together to witness the ceremony. There was policy too; for he wished them to go back impressed with the greatness of his power; and if any grieved at the loss of their national independence, he would make them understand how hopeless was resistance. What possibility could there be of shaking off the yoke of so mighty a conqueror! We may imagine him, therefore, casting his eyes all around, himself elated with the vastness of the concourse, of which every man represented some province or town, whose one despotic ruler was himself. Far and wide, throughout realms which but a short while ago had their own laws and native government, one will alone prevailed, one voice alone gave the law; and be it but the veriest whim or trifle, all those powerful satraps, and the provinces where they dwelt as kings, must bow their wills, and bend even their laws to gratify the mere passing fancy of their lord. There must be no hesitation, no questioning whether the command were just and right. It might be wrong and abominable, but that trained army, which that day celebrated its triumph, would enforce obedience. Where one man has despotic power, his subjects must not think that there are rights of conscience. Conscience grows and develops only where it is protected by equal laws; but it never attains to its full power except where there is a true religion, and men learn and feel that they must obey God rather than man.

But in the very hour of his exaltation, when to himself and to most of those who formed that mighty crowd, the sole thought was of the pride and majesty of the victorious king, strange news is brought to him. Some of his courtiers drew near, Chaldeans, men belonging to the dominant class at Babylon, and who therefore regarded Nebuchadnezzar's grandeur as reflecting splendour upon themselves; yet probably moved by meaner feelings. For the elevation of Jews to foremost rank was the bestowal upon aliens of what they regarded as belonging to themselves. Partly then as claiming to be especially loyal, and partly through grudge at the promotion of Daniel and his companions, they approached the king. They saluted him with the usual but extravagant wish of never-ending life, and after reciting his decree requiring universal prostration, and threatening all who refused with a most cruel death, they said, "There are certain Jews whom thou hast set over the affairs of the province of Babylon, Shadrach, Meshach, and Abed-nego; these men, O king, have not regarded thee: they serve not thy gods, nor worship the golden image which thou hast set up" (ver. 12).

Now it is probable that more than twenty years had passed since Daniel and his companions had been placed in a position of great influence; and during those twenty years Nebuchadnezzar had been establishing that first universal monarchy which Daniel had characterised as the head of gold. That dream and its interpretation had occurred about the year 603 B.C., while the date assigned to the setting up of the image is 580 B.C. We gather, therefore, that Daniel and his friends had long been faithfully discharging their duties to the king, keeping matters right at home while he was far away at the head of the army, governing the people justly and mercifully; but even by their upright administration making many enemies, who would gladly have seen men more manageable and more accessible to bribes and other corrupt influences at the head of affairs. And now these firm, righteous governors were in their power. They had disobeyed the king's command, and while all besides had prostrated themselves on the ground, they stubbornly had stood erect.

Every point in the accusation is put with telling force. They were officers in authority, and therefore bound to set an example of obedience. They owed their preferment to the royal favour, and were thereby, for very gratitude's sake, such as should have been foremost to do the king honour. They were aliens set over the nation, and it was their duty not to offend national prejudices. Nevertheless, they had shown no respect to the king; for they had not served his gods, nor prostrated themselves before the image he had set up.

No doubt this was the very view that Nebuchadnezzar would take, that it was an act of disrespect, and even of insult, to himself. For the image was but a symbol of his own glory, and the god was to be honoured because he had done his duty by his haughty worshipper. And as the day and the occasion was thus one of personal pride and boasting, it seemed to the king an act of treason and utterly unendurable that these officers, who owed everything to his favour, should dare to disregard his orders.

But what was it that made these three noble men risk life and all they had rather than bow themselves for a few moments upon the ground? It was from no disrespect to the king. Probably those many years of warfare had produced a hardening effect upon Nebuchadnezzar, and done much to make him that cruel and blood-stained tyrant which is the character given to him in history. But it was no protest against the king's degeneracy which made the Jewish young men disobey his command. They would have yielded a ready obedience if it had been possible. It was impossible. And why? Because it was not right.

Here we have one of the most precious results of a true religion. In false religions the character of God is so debased that His worship is of a feeble and temporising character. Only a true religion makes the uncompromising demand, "Thou shalt love the Lord thy God with all thy heart, and Him only shalt thou serve." It was no business of these Jews to judge Nebuchadnezzar and say, "Long possession of dictatorial power has done injury to thy moral character, and we will not obey a bad man." We find the apostles inculcating obedience to "the powers that be" at a time when a Nero was Emperor at Rome. And yet the Christians, while yielding a ready obedience, even to a Nero, refused apparently so slight a concession as burning a few grains of incense before the emperor's bust, and died rather than obey. The command was often urged upon them from motives of compassion, and their compliance made as easy as possible; but all in vain. They preferred death to submission; and Christendom has ever since crowned them with honour and regarded them as men worthy of endless praise. The Christian rule of conduct is obedience in all things innocent and lawful; but obedience to God first of all, and wherever earthly rulers command anything contrary to God's will, then "we ought to obey God rather than men" (Acts v. 29).

It is a painful question whether we nationally act up to this high standard. For the purpose of propitiating our heathen or Mohammedan fellow-subjects, our troops, or others whom we employ, are sometimes required to take part in processions and ceremonies in honour of false gods. Often it sorely tries the conscience of many a brave man, and he feels that his allegiance to his God is compromised by the command given to him by his officers. He feels that he, a Christian, is required to do that which these three noble Jews were willing to die rather than consent to do. Ought Christian rulers thus to violate the consciences of their subjects? Can that political expediency be right which humiliates those who worship the true God in order to conciliate men who worship idols?

Even if it did conciliate them, it would be to their real injury, because it would only bind more firmly around them the bonds of impure and unholy and debasing superstitions. But does it conciliate them? Does it not rather make them despise a nation which affects to give outward honour to that which it at the same time rejects as irrational and false?

There was a more manly firmness about these three Jews. They asserted that there was a difference between truth and falsehood, between right and wrong. And they acted in accordance with their professions.

They were Nebuchadnezzar's officers, and would gladly have obeyed his lawful commands. But he required them to do that which the law of God forbade. Jehovah had given His people in the Ten Commandments clear rules for their conduct. At the time when He spake them the laws of morality were but ill understood. Mercifully, God gave by the voice of inspiration a plain summary of duty, and the conscience of man has for more than three thousand years bowed before their might, and accepted them as a true embodiment of the laws of right and wrong. But for Shadrach, Meshach, and Abed-nego it was enough that they were the inspired declaration of the will of God, and as being His will, they were ready to obey at all hazards. Now two of these commandments forbade compliance with the king's orders. True that a thousand years had passed since they were enacted, and that circumstances had greatly changed. Were they, captives at Babylon, to give up positions of great usefulness, which God had given them providentially in order that they might soften the treatment of their brethren in exile—were they to abandon all this rather than bend their bodies for a minute with thousands of other men? They might have argued that they did not worship the image, but merely paid due respect to the king. They might have said that though they prostrated the body, the mind stood erect, and with it they worshipped only Jehovah. But they had recourse to no casuistry. Casuistry is too often only the art of finding excuses for evading the laws of God. These steadfast Jews felt that they must obey the laws of God in their simple and primary sense. They might have to die a painful and horrible death, but even so they felt that it was right to obey God rather than man.

There was no delay in pronouncing their doom; for we thus read, "Then Nebuchadnezzar in his rage and fury commanded to bring Shadrach,

Meshach, and Abed-nego. Then they brought these men before the king" (ver. 13).

Fierce was the conqueror's wrath; for their disobedience was an offence against himself. Still there was some degree of moderation in his conduct. He asks, "Is it true? Do not ye serve my gods?" More exactly the words mean, " Is it of set purpose, O Shadrach, Meshach, and Abed-nego, that ye serve not my gods, nor worship the golden image which I have set up?" (ver. 14.)

The king probably called to mind their long and faithful service; he may even have remembered Daniel's interpretation of his dream, and that he had promoted these men because of the extraordinary events at that time. But he may also have simply doubted whether such disobedience were possible. It may have seemed to him incredible that at such a time any one should dare to beard him, and disregard a command given under so terrible a penalty. There must be some mistake. They must have misunderstood his order; and so he repeats it to them. The varied strains of music shall again resound, and all shall stand about them and witness their obedience. "If ye fall down and worship the image which I have made; well: but if ye worship not, ye shall be cast the same hour into the midst of a burning fiery furnace; and who is that God that shall deliver you out of my hand?" (ver. 15).

These last defiant impious words show that the king had a suspicion that after all the act was a wilful one, and done for a religious reason. He knew that the Jews were unlike all other people. There was something about them very unbending and uncompromising, especially in matters of religion. They did not patronise their Deity as he patronised Nebo and Merodach, but obeyed Him, and were ready to suffer for His sake. For their God was the One God, holy, just, and true, who, though He will not clear the guilty, is merciful and compassionate; yet is He also supreme, and claims empire over all the earth. No people on earth besides held such views about their God.

Wonderful is the power of faith in one God, if that faith be no mere pantheistic fancy of a blind agency pervading nature, or of God being a universal spirit, of whom we ourselves are part, and into whose broad bosom we and all things return. The faith that has power is a belief in a personal God, who rewards and punishes (Heb. xi. 6). Of such a God Nebuchadnezzar had no idea, and in his arrogant challenge there was probably no conscious blasphemy. His gods were his servitors; and what could the Jewish Jehovah do more than

THE ACCUSATION. 113

Nebo and Merodach? The words express his proud conviction of his thorough superiority. And such a feeling was not without some justification. Nebuchadnezzar was more powerful than his gods. No doubt he supposed that they had some sort of power somewhere or other; but power over him they had little. They might help him, and ought to do so. If they neglected him, he might order their temples to be levelled to the ground, and forbid men henceforth ever to worship them. And if he thus acted, their priests would soon represent their gods as very humble and contrite, and would patch up a peace between them and their too-powerful votary. No heathen can really respect his gods, or care to imitate or obey them.

In our next study we will consider the noble answer of these three men. Let me now, in conclusion, say a few words upon the importance of right views of the nature of God. The degradation of the heathen world was greatly caused by the base and silly tenets of their religions. In Greece the gods were poetic beings, mere creatures of the fancy, and naturally, therefore, were pleasure-loving, licentious, and impure. Their worship was but a cloak for sin, and their festivals were but an occasion of shameless riot and wanton revelry. The gods of Rome were embodiments of the strong

H

elements of the national character, and did nothing to repress cruelty and violence or check the fierceness of their passions, but rather served to excuse or gild their lust for war. When subsequently they had attained to empire, their beliefs, if any remained, were but incentives to voluptuousness, the reaction from which was a stoical repression of all healthy and natural feeling. And in the East, with its deep under-current of melancholy and despair, religion was a blood-stained superstition, which did but deepen the gloom, and cause the worshipper in his misery to seek by the sacrifice of all he held most dear to propitiate cruel and insatiate demons. The religion of these three Jews was one that told them of God's universal empire, of His justice, and yet of His love. What comfort for these poor exiles at Babylon to know that even there the God whom they served was the sole King, without whose will nothing could happen in heaven or in earth. There can be no security on earth, no firm confidence in hours of difficulty and danger, unless there be above us one sovereign, almighty, eternal Lord, whose will is calmly and persistently carrying onwards His purposes of mercy and love.

These men too were suffering chastisement. Now, punishment usually hardens. The fear of it may deter from crime; but the offender who has been detected and punished generally loses all sense of shame, and is made fit for worse offences. But in God's dealings with His people in chastisement there is that which makes it healthful, and the spring of a regenerate life. The Jews in exile were made to feel that God was dealing with them in love. It was no blazing furnace of destruction into which they were cast; but they had been placed in the refiner's fire, in order that they might come forth all glorious and pure. It was not the hard scourge of tyrant or slave-owner that was giving them temporary pain; it was the gentle hand of a loving father: and so at Babylon the God who was punishing them was also their comfort and strength, and the sure rock of their confidence. Their thought was, that "like as a father pitieth his children, so Jehovah pitieth them that fear Him" (Ps. ciii. 13); and the whole nation turned in humility and penitence back to God, because they were sure that He loved them. And so was it with these three. They were sure that Jehovah loved them, and therefore even death was sweet if borne for His sake.

But, finally, there was that which gave strength and stability to their conduct. The pathway of life is not always strewn with rose-leaves; if it were, men should soon deteriorate into effeminate lovers of softness. There was a firm, stern centre to the faith of these Jews. God was loving and kind; but He was also just, and One who claims obedience. It is no true faith which is devoid of a deep sense of duty to God. There is nothing nobler in man than this sense of duty, and the determination firmly and manfully to obey God's law, and do what is right. The thought that made them bold and resolute was not so much the conviction that God is the universal King, as that He was their King. Come what would, in weal and woe, in the sunshine of prosperity and in the dark hours of imminent and painful death, they must obey God. He might save them; He might let them bring Him glory by their martyrdom. With this they had no concern. They must not be guided by regard to consequences. These they must leave to God. Their duty was to obey Him, and bear all that might follow, and brave danger, and pain, and death.

It was their firm faith that supported them in their trial. But it held them up because their religion was true, and gave them right and adequate ideas about God. And in this lies the importance of a true religion, that it raises and elevates men, and gives strength and nobleness to their lives.

Every corruption of our creed, every erroneous doctrine and perversion of view, is a distinct loss. As far as it goes it depresses our spiritual standard, enfeebles our conscience, takes away the inner bone from our characters, and makes us unequal to a firm and consistent walk with God. But a true and scriptural belief will not by itself suffice. There must be a living faith in the God which it sets before us. Many a Jew, it may be, prostrated himself before the image. These three did not, because to true doctrine there was added a firm real faith in the God whom their inspired Scriptures had made known to them.

VIII.

CALMNESS AND FURY.

(DANIEL iii. 16–23.)

"O NEBUCHADNEZZAR, we are not careful to answer thee in this matter." In the answer of the three Jewish young men to Nebuchadnezzar there is the same firm ring as in that given by St. Peter to the Jewish Sanhedrim, "We ought to obey God rather than men." In neither case was there any defiance or rudeness, though the king might regard any and all resistance to his orders as an act of rebellion. But there was the fearless statement that a higher authority existed than that of either king or sanhedrim, with the unflinching determination to yield obedience where it was due. If the king's command had not clashed with the law of God, the three Jewish officers would have obeyed it; for in all earthly matters the king's authority was real. But he had passed beyond the bounds of his legitimate rights and trespassed on those of God; and it was their duty, as it is the duty of all men, to "obey God and not men" wherever the two powers stand opposed to one another.

In our Version there is an appearance of rudeness, but it is because the word *careful* has changed its meaning. "To be careful" means now to take pains in a matter, and to be prudent and cautious. Now it would have been wrong to have been indifferent as to the form of their answer, or to have replied lightly, and so as to have irritated Nebuchadnezzar without reason. But when our Version was made, *careful* meant full of care, anxious; and so the words then rightly rendered, "Be careful for nothing" (Phil. iv. 6), are in the Revised Version now rightly rendered, "In nothing be anxious," because the meaning of the word has changed. So when Isaiah addresses the "careless daughters" of Jerusalem, no blame is intended in the word used by the prophet. Really it is equivalent to the "being at ease," and the persons addressed are the women of the wealthier classes, whose life was raised above anxiety for their daily wants.

Our translators therefore meant, "We are not anxious or distressed about our answer, but leave the matter calmly to God." This is not, however, the exact sense of the Chaldee in this place, which more accurately means, "It is not our business to answer thee, O king." It is not we on whom the matter rests. Really it belongs to God. And this sense is brought out more clearly by the correct translation of vers. 17, 18, "If our God, whom we serve, is able to deliver us from the furnace, He will deliver us; but if not, we still cannot obey thee, but prefer death to idolatry." This translation has probably been avoided, because it seems to imply a doubt in their minds as regards God's power to save; but such is not really the meaning. There is no wavering in their hearts, but the form of their language was settled by the opening words, that it was not their business to answer. They felt that faith in the existence of God was at stake. It was not a controversy between three Jewish captives and the mighty king whose slaves they were. The controversy was between belief in one supreme Almighty God and idolatry. It was thus God's matter, and He would settle it for Himself in His own way. They do not boast, and assert that necessarily their God could and would deliver them, but were willing that it should be put to the proof. Nevertheless they knew that God does not often interfere with human beings by direct intervention. From time to time His people have to honour Him by suffering for Him; and for this they were prepared. "But if not, that is, if God do not deliver us out of thy hands, then we are content to die." There was no doubt in their minds that God could save them; but they were not equally sure that He would. That must depend upon His good will and pleasure. And if He did not deliver them, they were ready to attest their allegiance to Him and their hatred of idolatry by dying rather than worship the image which the king had set up.

There was, then, in the words no determination to force God, as it were, to save them by a miracle. But there was, first of all, the exercise of free-will and choice. This is what St. Paul enjoins upon all Christians when he bids them "prove all things" (1 Thess. v. 21). And it is both a very noble and also a very serious thing. It is noble, because we exercise in it our gift of reason, that high faculty which distinguishes man from all other denizens of this world. But reason alone does not choose for us. Perhaps even it seldom chooses, but is employed to find causes, excuses, and pretences for conclusions arrived at without any careful examination whether they are right and true. What really chooses for us is our will. We decide according to our affections, our passions, our desires, and the influence of past actions and of habits already formed. And herein lies the serious side of our duty of making choice. Our happiness or misery in life, our peace or our ruin in eternity, depend upon the manner in which we here decide what shall be the motives on which we act, and what our conduct shall be.

It is in our thus having the power to decide for ourselves and choose as we will that our likeness to God and our being fashioned in His image consists. Our likeness to Him who is the great First Cause does not consist in our being endowed with reason, though reason is a Divine gift to aid us in making our choice aright. Nevertheless when Eve committed the first sin done upon earth she made use of her reason. She took the forbidden thing not idly, but because she " saw that the tree was good for food, and that it was pleasant to the eyes, and a tree to be desired to make one wise" (Gen. iii. 6). Every one of these three points was weighty. Not much weight perhaps in the matter of the supply of food for material wants, but much in its adding to the pleasure and refinement of life, and most of all in its leading to growth of knowledge and intellectual activity. Yet the taking of the fruit was a sin and the cause of terrible misery. For reason served her just as it serves us. It gave her a one-sided representation, and adduced only arguments and motives in favour of taking. The arguments for refraining it omitted. And this is ever the case. Reason is an advocate which makes the best of its own side. It does not choose its side, but is retained by other powers, and argues for a foregone conclusion. Eve wished for the fruit, and her reason gave her three good arguments in justification of taking it. So with us. In the hour of temptation and trial reason will not save us. We shall stand or fall according as our will decides for us, and reason will be the ready advocate to justify whatever we do.

What then can save us? Only the power of faith acting upon our will, and enabling us firmly to choose a life of duty. If there be no spiritual life in the soul, nothing there to sanctify the will, the brightest and clearest intellect may be humbled unto the service of sin and Satan. Now these three Jews were men who knew the power of faith, and they came into the king's presence with their minds fully made up upon the most momentous question which can occupy the heart of man. It is, in fact, the great alternative to be settled by us all. The purpose of this life plainly seems to be that we should in it choose between present pleasure and future happiness; between the life that now is and that which is to come; between God and the devil. And no man can make this choice aright except upon the motive of faith. No man can come to God unless he believe in the two primary articles of natural and all religion—first, that there is a God, and secondly, that God rewards and punishes human actions (Heb. xi. 6); and that consequently there is a right and a wrong in human conduct, and a future judgment, where the right will be rewarded and the wrong be punished.

Now Shadrach and his friends had long made up their minds upon this point. When quite young they had had the grace given them to choose the right and to reject whatever is contrary to God's will. They had lived long in the exercise of faith, both in there being a God, and also in His practical interference with the concerns of men. And hitherto, after one short trial, it had worked for their earthly good and happiness, as is the usual rule with the service of God. For "godliness," we are told, "has the promise of the life that now is, as well as of that which is to come" (1 Tim. iv. 8). They had enjoyed also the inward peace and happiness of believing, and of feeling that God was near them; but at length a change had come. Every man's work must be tried, and the hour of their trial had arrived; and its manner was most severe and terrible. But were the convictions of a life to be carelessly laid aside? Oh, no! The hour of trial, when a man is put into the refiner's fire, does not make him good metal, but it shows of what metal he is made, and separates in him the pure gold from the worthless dross.

And herein lies the importance of a true creed. Why is it that men like these Jews under the Old Testament dispensation, and Christians now and at all times, are ready to give up life and everything for God? Of all that vast concourse, representing the foremost nations of earth, only Jews were found willing to stake their lives upon their religion. But for Jews to do so was a matter of course. But why so? It is because a true religion is the sole thing which enlightens the conscience, and so trains and strengthens it as to invest it with real power in the guidance of our lives. We have seen that it is our will which decides for us, and we have in our natures such fierce passions, such lust after pleasure, and vanity, and gain, and in our wills such weakness and readiness to give way, that with St. Paul we cry out, "O wretched man that I am! who shall deliver me from the body of this death?" (Rom. vii. 24); for "in this tabernacle we do groan, being burdened, not for that we would be unclothed, and get rid of our bodies, but clothed upon, and invested with new and spiritual power, that what is mortal may be swallowed up of life" (2 Cor. v. 4). But when men have felt themselves thus "clothed upon," their will enlightened by Divine knowledge and sanctified by the Holy Spirit's indwelling, they then choose God's service so firmly and joyfully that no earthly terrors can shake or move them from their sure foundation.

This, then, is what religion does for us. It clothes us with power. Under false religions the conscience remains in a rudimentary state, and though it does approve or condemn, and say this is right and that wrong, it acts but weakly and ignorantly, and is a very feeble monitor. And with so little help men's lives sink down into mean baseness. But a true faith and the Holy Spirit's aid build up the conscience, and give it, first, light, whereby it distinguishes right and wrong clearly; and secondly, power, so that it speaks to the will with all authority, and says, "This thou shalt do, and this thou shalt leave undone." And thus Shadrach and his companions came into the king's presence as men who had long ago made their choice between duty and disobedience, between the service of God and a life of sin. They had never anticipated such a trial, nor supposed that their faith would be put to so severe a proof. Probably they would gladly have escaped from it could they have done so honourably, and without violating their conscience or abandoning their faith. This could not be, and therefore with calm sure trust in God they reply, "We have no need to answer thee in this matter. It is a matter belonging to God. If He be able, in accordance with the laws of His righteous governing, He will deliver us from this fiery death. But if He do not deliver us, we cannot and will not serve idols. For by so doing we should violate our convictions of what is right and wrong." Conscience had long ago decided for them what their lives were to be. And under its influence they could not abandon the faith which had enlightened the conscience and given it this power; nor could they be false to that God who had been their peace and happiness, and whom they knew to be the sole Almighty Governor both in heaven above and in earth below.

Calm as was their answer, yet there was in it that which enraged the king to madness. There was the assertion of the existence of a power higher than his own, the claim to act according to the conscience, and the resolute determination to obey the law of God rather than that of man. To Nebuchadnezzar Jehovah was one of the many gods whom he had vanquished. Like Sennacherib of old, his boast was that "his hand had taken kingdoms whose idols were far superior to any deity worshipped at Jerusalem, and that he had done to Jerusalem and her idols as he had done to those of other conquered towns" (Isa. x. 10, 11). And yet these captive Jews, the vessels of whose God were exhibited in the temple of Bel as trophies of Jehovah's defeat, were resolutely declaring their determination to obey Him rather than pay even a passing homage to the god of the victor. Such audacity must be signally punished, and therefore the furnace must be heated seven times more than usual, and the most mighty men of his army must bind the offenders and cast them into the flames.

"Seven times more than it was wont to be heated." There is a dreadful significance about these words. They show that this was the ordinary form of capital punishment when the king was displeased. And this is confirmed by what we read in the Book of Jeremiah, that it became a form of curse at Babylon to say, "The Lord make thee like Zedekiah and like Ahab, whom the king of Babylon roasted in the fire" (Jer. xxix. 22). It was a cruel and barbarous method of destroying life, and happily now, if life has to be taken, the manner is made as little painful as possible. But

Christian martyrs have suffered even greater cruelties, and the rage shown against them down to the fires of Smithfield has been even more heartless and diabolical.

But the king's command was obeyed. The most famous of Nebuchadnezzar's warriors seized and bound the unresisting Jews. Probably they were chosen for this office because the day was one in honour of the king's conquests, and the refusal of these Jews to do homage to the idol was regarded as an insult to the army. Men, therefore, "mighty of strength," who by their prowess and vast physical powers had contributed to many a victory, were just the persons to punish this disrespect to themselves and their fellow-warriors. Probably, too, they entered with zest upon their office, and rejoiced in thus crushing these audacious contemners of their deeds.

At once they seize upon them. The king's commandment was urgent. There is no time for delay, or for clothing them in funereal garments. They bind them in their ordinary dress, of which the chief article was a loose flowing linen robe, and therefore of a highly inflammable nature. The furnace had to it a door or mouth (vers. 26), probably above, through which the victims were thrown down into the flames. Usually this could

I

be done without danger, but at the king's order large quantities of fuel had been cast into the furnace, and it was burning with the utmost violence. Probably, even, to make it seven times hotter than usual, oil and naphtha had been poured upon the flames; and when the mighty men carried their victims to the mouth of the oven the fumes suffocated them. It would be a painless death; for smoke and even blazing vapour admitted into the lungs immediately destroy all sensation. And that which destroyed the executioners would also naturally, with equal suddenness, have destroyed their victims. But the power of God was present to save. It was His matter, and He there gave to the heathen king a proof of His omnipotence.

But the miracle was not wrought for Nebuchadnezzar's sake. There is in the Bible a very sparing use of miracles until He came who was Himself the Incarnate God. There was no interference to save the Maccabean martyrs from the fury of Antiochus Epiphanes, but here Shadrach and his friends were saved. Neither was their faith stronger, nor their conduct more noble, than that of Samona and Eleazar; but they were saved, and saved miraculously, because the occasion made it, if we may reverently so speak, necessary. With Jerusalem in ruins, the temple burnt with fire, the people in exile and wasted to a remnant, it was essential to the continuance of the Church upon earth, and to the belief in a personal God, that the faith of the Jews at Babylon should be confirmed. And God did confirm it by rescuing His servants from the violence of the king.

But with what terror must the poor exiles have watched the proceedings, and how deep must have been their despair as they saw the Chaldean warriors bind for execution the men who had for so many years been their friends and protectors! And probably many a prayer went up to heaven in their behalf; but here and there, it may be, some scoffer, false to his faith, said derisively, "See to what an end faith brings them!" Just one prostration among thousands of prostrate forms, and they would have retained their high offices, have saved their lives, and been able still to work for their nation. But faith does not judge by human standards of action. It raises men up so high that their vision extends far and wide to things that worldly men see not. And therefore their judgment is more true because more falls within the range of their sight. The man who sees this earth alone, this life alone, the body only, he sees but the smaller and less worthy half. How can he judge aright to whom the soul, with all its hopes and aspirations, its longings for immortality, and for the heavenly life promised to it, counts for nothing? Compared with us these Jews lived but in the twilight. The Sun of Righteousness had not arisen to shine on them in its meridian splendour. But they had the light of dawn, and it showed them the pathway of safety.

They set to us a bright example. In the fulness of their powers, in the vigour of manhood, in the possession of high office, and with so much to make the life even of an exile happy, they deliberately placed their duty to God first. And God accepted their devotion to His service, and raised them to a position of even greater earthly usefulness and of more exalted spirituality. The lamp of their faith, cleared of all earthly impurity by their devotion in the hour of trial, burned ever more brightly, and their light affliction wrought for them an exceeding weight of glory. And these things are written for our instruction, that we may in our measure imitate and follow the example of God's honoured saints of old.

IX.

THREE JEWISH CONFESSORS.

(DANIEL iii. 24–30.)

IN the previous narrative we have seen the brave spirit of these holy martyrs, ready to yield their bodies to a cruel death rather than be false in their allegiance to their God. We have seen, too, what strength there is in the belief in one God. There can be no confidence nor firm trust where men suppose that there is a multitude of gods. For one god may have to yield to another, or may find his power limited by another's dominion. The Greeks of old believed that there were quarrels and feuds and divisions among the inhabitants of their Olympus, and that one deity might have to sacrifice the interests of his devotees in order to obtain some concession for other favourites. Happy was Israel of old in the belief in one God, and many were the deeds of heroism wrought in the strength of this conviction.

Nor can there be peace of mind and calm fortitude where the one god is the mere sum of the being of the universe. To the pantheist God is not a Person, omniscient, omnipresent, almighty, who sees and knows and takes interest in all he does. To him God is a blind power, the mere aggregate of the working of nature and man, of whom he is himself part, and into whom he will finally be absorbed. Such a deity has no separate existence, no separate action, no separate knowledge, no personal will, no special sphere of duty. The man may see, but the god, who is the mere sum of all human and animal seeing, himself sees not. Man may work, and nature may employ her physical and vegetative energies, but the sum of all this working can do nothing. Whatever it be, it has not even an existence for and in itself, and can inspire no hope, can give man no courage in danger, no consolation in sorrow, no strength for right action. Such a god is a name, and not a being, and there is no such thing as responsibility to him. And absorption into him at death simply means the ceasing to have a separate existence. In life we are the acting, thinking, energising part of the pantheistic god; to be absorbed into him at death is to fall into unconsciousness.

In neither polytheism nor pantheism is there any nobleness of thought, or anything to make man better and aid him in becoming godlike on earth. It is responsibility to an almighty, omniscient, and just Judge which raises man to the true height of his dignity, as a being endowed by God with free will and a conscience; and the answer to the question why God has made this world such as it is, and placed man in a position so full of difficulty, is to be found in the thought, that only by bearing the burden of responsibility can man be made fit for God's service in heaven. Here, on earth, men rise in moral worth and social influence by responsibility rightly borne; and the whole doctrine of a future judgment, and of eternal rewards and punishments, has for one great purpose the impressing the minds of men with a sense that they are responsible to a righteous Judge for all they think and say and do.

It was this sense of responsibility to a personal God which gave these three Jewish martyrs their high courage, their strength to resist a despotic monarch, their calmness and joy in the hour of suffering. And on the other side we see the king, possessed of every earthly splendour and greatness, a warrior crowned with constant victory, a statesman who had built up a mighty empire, the absolute master of every then known country, without a rival upon earth, but with no sense of responsibility either to God or man; and his history shows us that there was little happiness for one so situated. We shall see him, hereafter, the victim of a strange mental malady, caused by excessive pride and passions unrestrained. In this chapter we see him given over to vanity. He celebrates his triumph by making an image, destitute, apparently, of all beauty, and remarkable only for its size and costliness. And all men must come and worship this image, not for the honour of God, but to minister to the pride of man. And vanity is succeeded by rage and ill-temper. He finds among his officers three who will not bow the knee. Thousands of men, of whom many were far higher in rank and dignity, were content to bow; were ready to submit to any degradation in order to please their despotic master. But what was that as long as there was found upon earth one man who had a will of his own, and who dared to say that anything whatsoever that was commanded was sinful, and that he would obey God rather than the king? And so cruelty followed upon vanity and anger. The furnace must be heated seven times more fiercely than usual; his mightiest men must throw these rebels into the flames; and the king, in his chair of state, sits opposite the furnace, that he may see his wrath wreaked upon the offenders.

There could be no happiness, no inward content and peace of mind, for a man whose heart was the den wherein such fierce passions dwelt. The base, unholy monsters kennelled there would sooner or later tear him to pieces, like another Actæon, hunted and pulled down by his own hounds.

But what does the king see? First, his own favourite officers slain by the heat of the fire. That, probably, gave but a momentary vexation, and only made him more wrathful against the offending Jews. But soon he sees another sight. "Then Nebuchadnezzar the king was astonied, and rose up in haste, and spake, and said unto his counsellors, Did not we cast three men bound into the midst of the fire? They answered and said unto the king, True, O king. He answered and said, Lo, I see four men loose, walking in the midst of the fire, and they have no hurt; and the form of the fourth is like the Son of God."

He had seated himself upon his throne to see his sentence put into execution. Around him stood his senators and the great officers of state. The three martyrs had spoken about their God being able to deliver them out of the king's hand; but their words had seemed to him but as insolence, and as the defiant words of rebels. Little did he dream of there being any deliverance for them.

They stood alone, powerless, without earthly aid or helper; and even this may have increased the king's anger at what seemed such empty bravado of his royal dignity. But a strange sight now meets his eye. The three offenders remain unhurt, though the heat had slain his officers. They had been cast into the furnace bound; now some unseen power has loosed their bands. They are free; are walking unhurt in the midst of the flames, and with them is a Divine companion. The words of Nebuchadnezzar literally mean "a son of the gods." He knew nothing of the doctrine of a Messiah, or of the Divine Son coming down to earth to bear our nature. But he saw in the furnace a fourth being, of a grand and noble presence, who seemed to him evidently more than man. He may even have thought that it was the tutelary deity of fire, who had manifested himself in the midst of the flames. For the Babylonians worshipped fire as a god, and celebrated him as born of the ocean, whence he raises himself on high, to illumine the darkness and to chase evil away.

But more probably the king meant only that this fourth person seen in the midst of the fire was a grand and glorious being, whose presence filled him with awe. Had the three Jewish youths merely escaped, that would have been marvellous; but the presence of this fourth person proved that their deliverance was Divine. And as he gazed, Nebuchadnezzar remembered their words. They had cast scorn on his gods, and declared that their God was able to deliver them. And He had delivered them. And the king felt that there was a mightier power at work, ordering things on earth, than he had imagined. He might be the greatest of earthly kings, but the god in whose honour he had set up his colossal image was not the greatest of all gods, for the God of the Jews had vanquished him. And Nebuchadnezzar frankly acknowledges the defeat. With all his faults, there was much about him that was admirable, and made him not altogether unworthy to be, in the words of Jeremiah, Jehovah's servant. He descends therefore from his throne, and goes to the mouth of the furnace, and cries, "Shadrach, Meshach, and Abed-nego, ye servants of the most high God, come forth and come hither." It does not follow that he recognised Jehovah as his own God. The minds of the heathen were in strange confusion as to the Godhead. Doctrines that to us seem elementary, and are understood and regarded as necessary truths even by children, were above their comprehension. For idolatry debases the mind, and so does any system which places saints or human mediators in the place of deity. If they can hear the prayers of their worshippers, they must be omnipresent, and to be omnipresent they must each be God. It was this multitude of gods which made heathen worship minister only to human weakness and folly, and even to sin. And Nebuchadnezzar, brought up in this insensate system, acknowledged no more than that the God of the three martyrs was one of surpassing majesty. There was many a long road to be traversed before he could attain to a belief so noble and sublime as that God is one.

And now in wonder they all examine these men. On one side the dead bodies of the officers who had cast them into the furnace, scorched and withered by the heat, testified that the flames had not lost their power. On the other side stood "these men, upon whose bodies the fire had no power, nor was an hair of their head singed, neither were their coats changed, nor the smell of fire had passed on them." Again and again they examine them. First and chief the king; but the rest with eager curiosity press around. So strange is the sight that they cannot satisfy their eyes with looking. They feel their bodies, touch their clothes, examine their very hair, and smell their garments, and can trace no influence upon them of fire. Then they turned to the dead bodies. Why are these alive and unhurt, and those slain? What had made the difference? What was it that had so changed the power of the fire?

Throughout it had been a religious ordeal. The three Jewish youths had stood alone against the king's command, and they had dared to disobey, not as disloyal to the king, but because they would not serve the king's god. From first to last it had been clearly shown that it was duty, duty and obedience to their own Jehovah, that had moved and forced them to the deed. And their God had interfered for them and delivered them. But martyrs usually have to die for their religion. Why had God rescued these?

A miracle is never wrought without some necessary reason. It would be contrary to God's wisdom to interfere with the ordinary course of nature and with natural laws unless the occasion justified the interference. Here we seem to see reasons which did justify it. For the Jews were the depositaries of revealed religion. To them had been intrusted the oracles of God. And usually they had been protected by a special providence. But now all care of them seemed gone. Their temple was burnt, their kings slain, their priests and people carried into captivity. If they had proved unworthy of their trust before, great was the danger lest they should now fall quite away, and revealed religion cease to have a local home and guardians. But God wonderfully interfered in their behalf. They saw Daniel and the three Jewish youths placed in high office, and not only had they friends in them, but examples to strengthen their faith and encourage them in keeping true allegiance to Jehovah. And now their God had miraculously delivered their three protectors from imminent danger, and from the wrath of the king. We know from history that the exile at Babylon was a time of revival of true religion. Great had been the sins, and greater still the indifference of the nation in past time to the preciousness of the great trust committed to its keeping. At Babylon it awoke from its apathy, shook off its old coldness, and Israel became a nation strongly impressed with the sense of its high calling, earnest in its own faith and trust in its God, and eager to spend itself in His service.

Great and widespread was the influence of this miracle in working this mighty change; for the knowledge of it was not confined to the vast assemblage gathered on the plain of Dura. Even they would have carried the news home to every part of the empire. But the king was not content with this. By a solemn decree he made it known publicly and authentically to all his subjects. For so we read: "Then Nebuchadnezzar spake, and said, Blessed be the God of Shadrach, Meshach, and Abed-nego, who hath sent His angel and delivered His servants that trusted in Him, and have changed the king's word, and yielded their bodies, that they might not serve nor worship any god except their own God. Therefore make a decree, That every people, nation, and language, which speak anything amiss against the God of Shadrach, Meshach, and Abed-nego, shall be cut in pieces, and their houses shall be made a dunghill: because there is no other God that can deliver after this sort."

The decree goes no further than to declare that the God of Israel had displayed a power and a regard for His worshippers such as no other god could have done. It is the decree of one who still remained a worshipper of many gods. But with what delight must the words have been read in the homes of many a poor exile! He had seemed to have lost all; country, city, temple, freedom, national existence, religion, all seemed gone. But no! Religion, the best of all, was not gone. The king himself testified to their God being greater and better than his gods. Yea, God Himself had proved it. For when the three martyrs, trusting in Him, had disobeyed the king's command and prepared to die rather than swerve from their allegiance to Jehovah, He had sent His angel and delivered His servants.

It must have been great happiness to them to know that those who so often before had helped and protected them were "promoted," raised to greater dignity and influence " in the province of Babylon." But their chief joy would lie in their greater trust in God; for they would see in the miracle far more than the king had seen. Religion is the mainstay of daily life. Other feelings, which powerfully influence men, are called forth occasionally, and only from time to time, perhaps at distant intervals, do they agitate and move us to action. Religion is a daily and hourly influence. Like the air we breathe, we need it each minute. We rise in the morning to an unblessed life, unless we begin with the prayer for God's guidance, and go forth to our duties as work to be done for Him. We meet the trials and difficulties of the day calmly if only we feel that God is at our side. We lie down to rest cheerful and at peace, if we can look upward with quiet assurance, as knowing that He who has led us by day will guard our sleeping hours. Now it was this home influence of religion that would derive strength and vigour from the king's decree. The exiles would not expect miracles to be wrought for them, but they would feel sure that the watchful Providence of God was keeping guard over them. Their outward lot was sad enough; but there was comfort in their hearts. They had not lost everything as long as their God was with them. Did not the king himself say " that no other god could deliver after this sort"? And would He not show them mercy? Mercy for their own selves and for those whom they loved? Mercy also for their nation, and restoration, in due time, to their dear land?

This miracle, then, was one of the many causes which wrought so great a change in the moral and religious state of the people of Israel. And it is recorded for our instruction. No word of Holy Scripture is of mere temporary efficacy. Some parts of God's Word work more actively at one time, and other parts spring into new force and vigour at another. But it is all of it eternal, like the Giver. And God, who manifested His power so marvellously at Babylon, is equally ready to aid and strengthen and bless now. He suits His working to the time; but in every hour of need He will help all and each of His faithful servants. And He aided these three Jewish martyrs because their faith in Him was real. They were ready even to die for their God. There may be faith as firm and true now, and if so, it will assuredly be equally blest; or faith may be feeble and unsteady. If so, God may send trial and difficulty to sift and prove it. Happy are those who read Holy Scripture for the perfecting of their faith, and draw from each narrative its proper lesson. And if such feel that their faith is still feeble and unworthy to be compared with that of the saints of old, let them bring it to God's footstool and pray for greater strength, firmer courage, and for power to work for God because they love God; and their prayers will be heard, and they will be " promoted " in the service of the King of Heaven.

X.

HEATHEN RECOGNITION OF GOD.

(DANIEL iv. 1–9.)

WE have in this chapter a remarkable confession made by the greatest of the Babylonian monarchs, and interesting, not merely on account of the high qualities of the person who humbles himself in it, but also because it is the record of God's providence specially manifesting itself to a heathen. There have been theologians who have regarded the heathen world as lying outside the direct influences of God's Spirit, and as having a claim to nothing more than that general care which God bestows upon the realm of Nature as the Creator. We find in Nebuchadnezzar a heathen to whom special revelations were made; and in this present narrative the object was personal. Elsewhere the good of God's people, or the preparation for the kingdom of the Messiah, was the object for which the revelation was made; and there is in the Bible a wonderful diversity in the outward form and manner in which the one purpose of God was steadily carried forward, until "the fulness of time had come." But here we have a special interposition of God's Providence, and a revelation made in a dream, for the sake of a heathen. A man outside the privileged pale of the Church is found not to be outside the pale either of God's ordinary mercies or of exceptional privileges.

Apparently an interval of several years had elapsed between the deliverance of the three Jewish youths from the flames, recorded in chapter iii., and the king's humiliation narrated in this chapter. For the setting up of the image in the plain of Dura was the conqueror's thanksgiving to his gods for his many victories, and his act of self-glorification for success in war. Here we find him equally triumphant in the arts of peace. Babylon had for centuries been oppressed by the kings of its rival, Nineveh. It had attained to freedom under Nabopolassar, the father of Nebuchadnezzar, and for the limited period of seventy years was to be the golden head of the world. And Nebuchadnezzar made it worthy of its pre-eminence. After a wonderful career of rapid victory, he was dwelling "at rest in his house," with every enemy and rival vanquished; and during this interval of peace he had turned the whole power of his genius to the fortifying and embellishing of his capital. In the cuneiform inscriptions we find numerous references made to his buildings, and even hymns of praise used at their dedication. And this is especially the case with the royal palace, which surpassed all other edifices in extent and grandeur, and in the costliness of its decorations. The Arabs now call it Mujalibé, "the overturned;" and all that remains of its magnificence is a heap of unsightly ruins.

It was then in its first glory, and Nebuchadnezzar had dwelt for several years in peace in his kingdom. During this period Daniel had been the king's vizier (Dan. v. 11), and in the transaction of business had necessarily been often brought into close contact with the sovereign. It is in this intercourse of many years that we find the explanation of the more advanced views and riper knowledge of the nature of God, manifested in this document. We have often before pointed out that Nebuchadnezzar, even in his most pious moments, still thought and spake as a heathen. Nor has he altogether outgrown his heathenism even now. He describes Daniel as called Belteshazzar, after the name of his god, and as having within him the spirit of the holy gods (vers. 8, 9, 18). "The sentence, also, is by the decree of the watchers and the matter by the word of the holy ones" (ver 17), in accordance with the Babylonian mythology which gave to inferior gods the right to sit in council, and advise those who alone had the power to will and do.

But though he has not escaped from the meshes of heathenism, the king's heart is opening to higher truths. He has caught a glimpse of the unity of the Divine nature, and sees one God enthroned high above his gods, and ruling with supreme authority over all the kingdoms of the earth. We have seen before that the king felt himself to be more powerful than his deities, and regarded them as servitors who must do his bidding. If a god disobeyed him, could he not put his priests to death, and level his temples to the ground? Aye! that was a thing he had more than once commanded, and who could disobey him? But now he acknowledges that far above all watchers and holy ones is the "Most High, who ruleth in the kingdom of men, and giveth it to whomsoever He will, and setteth up over it the meanest of men." There is a ring, too, of inspired truth in the ascription of praise in verse 34, where the king "blesses the Most High, and praises and honours Him that liveth for ever, whose dominion is an everlasting dominion, and His kingdom from generation to generation." This admixture is just what we should expect to find in a man who was moving up into higher and purer realms of thought. He was leaving his old and debased notions, but he had not shaken himself free from them. There are commentators who have discussed at weary length the question of the authorship of Nebuchadnezzar's proclamation. Its doctrines are not so strictly monotheistic as for it to have been written by Daniel. There is too near an approach to monotheism for it to have had a heathen for its author. But Nebuchadnezzar was no mere heathen. He had been taught in a very wonderful way, and had learned very strange lessons. Surely it is blindness not to see in the narrative a most interesting study and disclosure of the state of Nebuchadnezzar's mind, after his reason had returned to him and he had reflected upon the chastisement which had befallen him. The Nebuchadnezzar of this chapter is not the fierce young king who, in all the pride of victory, was ready to burn men alive, and throw into a furnace any who dared resist him. It is an old man, whose reason has been obscured, who has been driven from men, and who has drank the cup of humiliation to the last dregs. But not in vain. He is a better man, more modest, more thoughtful; and if he has not passed over the threshold and entered God's temple of light, he is very near it, and sees something of the brightness of the truth revealed within. Let us hope that he did pass over it, and learned that the Most High was a God of love and mercy as well as of might and power and chastisement.

Addressing then *all peoples, nations, and languages, that dwell in all the earth*—for he supposed that his kingdom was conterminous with the whole inhabited world—he commences, as is usual in all Oriental proclamations, with a good wish: that *peace might be multiplied*, or increased richly, *unto them*. And then proceeds (ver. 2): "I thought it good to show the signs and wonders that the High God hath wrought toward me." Probably we must not press upon *signs*, as used here, the meaning which the word generally bears in the Bible, where it is equivalent to our modern word *miracle*. Even so it strictly signifies the sign which God gives of His presence in the affairs of men, and especially with reference to His great purpose of bestowing upon them a Saviour. Here it means a warning that some event of especial importance is about to happen; and such signs naturally are *wonders*. Whenever God draws near to man, the contrast between the finite and the Infinite, the All-powerful and human feebleness, necessarily fills man with awe.

The doxology, therefore, which follows in verse 3, is a natural outburst of praise. But in this case it is more than natural. The king had just been himself the object both of the chastising hand and of the love of the Most High. It was the confession, therefore, of a great truth, which nothing less than a Divine interposition had wrung from him.

He goes on to tell what especially were the signs and wonders which had thus forced him to confess the universal rule of one Almighty God: "I Nebuchadnezzar was at rest in mine house, and flourishing in my palace."

The words show that the long period of Nebuchadnezzar's wars was over. He was no longer a general at the head of his army, moving from place to place, to spread misery and rapine and ruin. It is to Nebuchadnezzar's credit that he could thus "rest in his house." The annals of the Assyrian kings represent them as regarding war as their pastime. It seemed to them mere hunting, only instead of wild beasts their victims were men. Nebuchadnezzar could occupy his mind with other things, and those not voluptuous like the pursuits ascribed to Sardanapalus, but of a more ennobling kind. His processes for peopling his huge city were cruel enough; but at least he provided for its security and prosperity.

The word translated *flourishing* is worth a moment's pause. Literally it is *green*, covered with fresh verdure. The Sacred Tree, an emblem borrowed from the Tree o Life in Paradise, is constantly found engraved on Babylonian gems and signets. We find in this dream the king compared to a tree, and the idea, moreover, is a Biblical one. Isaiah describes the army of Sennacherib as a forest, and his princes as trees of tall stature (Isa. x. 33, 34). Ezekiel compares the Assyrian to a cedar of Lebanon (Ezek. xxxi. 3). And the Messiah is likened to a sucker, in which the cut-down stem of Jesse revives, and grows once again into majesty (Isa. xi. 1).

But from the calmness of his repose the king is suddenly roused up: "I saw a dream which made me afraid, and the thoughts upon my bed and the visions of my head troubled me" (ver. 5). He had been startled in a similar way before (chap. ii. 1), and, doubtless, we are to understand that the dream was followed by anxious thoughts, which the king could not shake off. The confused images of dreams usually pass quickly away. A few minutes of the light of day suffice to put to flight the feeble memories of our half-waking imaginations. But this dream was no mere effect of uneasy slumbers. God had sent it for a purpose, and therefore He would not let it slip into oblivion. Troubled waking thoughts followed, and the king, agitated and ill at ease with the foreboding of coming danger, sends for the wise men of his kingdom to set his mind at rest.

It is remarkable that the king looks for help to the quarter where he had looked before in vain. But on this occasion he had not forgotten his night vision, and might suppose that with their great learning and many books on magic the astrologers could at least interpret a dream, though they could not discover it. It was their office to do so, and possibly they had interpreted many omens and signs and astral appearances in the intervening years. They fail, but the king does not order their instant execution, and the razing of their houses to the ground. The fierce heat of youth has burned itself out. He has learned to be more reasonable. It is said that the word *impossible* did not exist in Napoleon's dictionary. Nebuchadnezzar had learned that power has its limits, and that it is childish ignorance not to know the bounds of the possible and impossible; of what a ruler may reasonably expect, and what it is wrong and unreasonable to require.

There may be another reason for the king's calmness. When the Chaldeans failed before he was angry, because he believed in them, and expected that they would succeed. He had a better judgment now, and as they went through their formulæ, and made their calculations, and did everything in the most approved style of their art, and yet could give no reasonable answer, the sole result was that the king grew impatient for the man who never had failed, and so "at the last Daniel came in before me." He had become a great political officer, occupied with weighty affairs of state, and not to be sent for except in case of extremity. It shows strange ignorance of the etiquette of Oriental courts to suppose that one so high in rank as Daniel would be summoned in the first instance, and before the ordinary means for answering the king's question had been tried and failed. There is a manifest tone, moreover, of apology in Nebuchadnezzar's speech, which shows that Daniel was no longer holding the modest position which belonged to him in chapter ii. The king was an absolute despot, but even tyrants learn to control themselves in their behaviour towards men whose services are indispensable and necessary for the existence of their thrones. The good government and stability of the king's empire depended largely upon Daniel's wisdom, and though as "chief of the magicians" he might finally be appealed to, yet the king never forgets his rank.

Respectfully he addresses him: "O Belteshazzar, master of the magicians, because I know that the spirit of the holy gods is in thee, and no secret troubleth thee, tell me the visions of my dream that I have seen, and the interpretation thereof."

Evidently the king had sent for soothsayers, astrologers, and Chaldeans, because it was the right thing, and customary to do so. It would have been a slight put upon an influential body of men, greatly respected of the multitude, if he had passed them by. But he knew that he had something more trustworthy to fall back upon. And so he listens quietly to their feeble evasions, feels no disappointment at their failure, and sending for one well tried and highly valued, knows that there will be no mistake with him. "The spirit of the holy gods was in Daniel." The form of expression is heathenish. He still supposes that a multitude of deities exists. But he supposes that they have found in Daniel a home, and that his wisdom is no mere human foresight, no acuteness of quickened perception, no mere penetration of an understanding cleared from prejudices and half-truths. It is a Divine wisdom, inspired by the indwelling of the gods, and therefore no secret could trouble him. An experienced man may make a happy guess at the future: nothing less than Divine power can bestow the gift of prophecy.

In the next chapter we will consider the dream itself. In this we have seen that the effect of Daniel's piety and godliness had been to win for him a secure place in the heart and judgment of a man so great and highly endowed as Nebuchadnezzar. Not only had God preserved him in danger, but raised him to power and high estimation. And thus the few words of Holy Scripture now considered give us a twofold lesson — the lesson, first, of God's faithfulness to His people; and next, the lesson that those who trust in Him may be tried indeed, and have many a danger to encounter, but that their end will be peace and joy in believing.

XI.

A WATCHER AND A HOLY ONE.

(Daniel iv. 10-18.)

A FRESH interest has been given within the last few years to everything connected with Assyria and Babylonia, by the discovery of the libraries of Assyrian kings, buried beneath the mounds which mark the sites of forgotten cities that were famous of old. And as the ordinary writing material consisted of clay, formed either into tablets or cylinders, on which the letters were impressed, and which were then usually baked, these literary remains, though often broken and mutilated, are otherwise as legible as when first written. But it was only gradually that these cylinders could be understood; for at first neither the character nor the language was known. By the patient labours, however, of devoted men, all difficulties have been, by slow degrees, overcome. And now, though here and there words and phrases occur not entirely intelligible, yet generally, Assyrian and Babylonian inscriptions are as capable of translation as inscriptions in the Greek or Latin language.

A remarkable class of these cuneiform inscriptions runs parallel to the earlier portion of the Book of Genesis, and in it the sacred tree, representing the Tree of Life in Paradise, holds an important place. In the engravings of Botta and Layard we see this tree adored by royal personages, guarded by sacred beings, who stand by it in an attitude of veneration, while over it is the winged disk, which is the symbol of the Supreme Deity. As this holy tree is one of the most common figures on gems and among the ornaments even of buildings, it was certainly well known to Nebuchadnezzar; and as there was no idea in his mind that he was the person signified, we must not accuse him of pride in arrogating so sacred a symbol to himself. It was Daniel who supplied the interpretation : what the king saw was the sacred tree growing, and spreading forth its branches on every side.

But the image was perfectly natural in itself; and while the ancients do not seem to have cared much for the larger beauty of the landscape, they greatly admired noble trees. Herodotus describes Xerxes as decking with ornaments of gold a splendid plane-tree which he passed on his march. Similar feelings are expressed by many classic authors. Virgil makes his shepherds recline under a spreading beech; Horace loved the elm and the poplar festooned around with vines; and in the Bible Abraham chooses an oak grove for his habitation. Deborah dwells beneath a palm; while Saul holds his court under a tamarisk-tree (1 Sam. xxii. 6); and beneath another tamarisk, as a tree loved by him while living, his bones, and those of Jonathan his son, were laid at rest (ibid. xxxi. 13).

We find, moreover, trees often playing a foremost part in dreams. Many are the instances mentioned: let me add one more. When Ephrem, the Syrian poet, was a child, he dreamed that out of his tongue there sprouted a vine, which grew till it reached to heaven, and produced leaves and fruit in endless abundance. All creation came and gathered of its clusters, and none went away unfilled. On his death-bed, in his last words to his weeping friends, he tells them this dream, and interprets it of his hymns, which were at that time learned by heart and sung by all the Christians in the East.

The metaphor of the tree, then, was natural in itself, and especially appropriate at Babylon, where sculptured on every side was the Tree of Paradise. Moreover, in its grandeur and magnificence it was a fit representation of the king, described before as the golden head of earthly monarchy. For "the tree grew, and was strong, and the height thereof reached unto heaven, and the sight thereof to the end of all the earth: the leaves thereof were fair, and the fruit thereof much, and in it was meat for all: the beasts of the field had shadow under it, and the fowls of the heaven dwelt in the boughs thereof, and all flesh was fed of it" (vers. 11, 12).

How grand a picture is this of an empire self-contained and producing within itself all that it needed. There is in it no feeling of insecurity; no dread of poverty or want. Food is found therein enough for all. Trade, agriculture, art, science, all flourish, and none who come to its ruler are sent away with their manifold needs unsatisfied. It is also a kingdom that develops itself and extends its influence on every side. Now if this growth had been natural, like that of a tree, all had been well. And a righteous kingdom would thus grow and expand. The cause of war and fighting among nations is the same as that which produces discord among individuals. Men quarrel because they all seek their own, and not another's good. But a nation loving and practising righteousness would be at peace within itself, and strong, therefore, to resist foreign aggression; while it would provoke no ill-will, and would conciliate trust and affection. We condemn these ancient empires for their lust of war; and yet Christendom, after long centuries of nominal allegiance to "the Prince of Peace," lives in an armed preparedness almost as disastrous as war.

Thus the vision bears witness to the great qualities of Nebuchadnezzar as a ruler. His civil administration must have been as vigorous and wise as had been his government in war, or it would not have been possible to represent his empire under an image so descriptive in every particular of prosperity, and of the contentment of all classes of his subjects.

"Now as he gazed upon the sacred tree, behold a watcher and a holy one came down from heaven." The word watcher, *'iro*, became an ordinary term in the Syrian Church for angel, and Ephrem Syrus classes the *watchers* with the Seraphim and Cherubim as a special order of heavenly beings. The use, however, of the word in the Syrian Church was probably borrowed from this passage, and it is interesting to find in the Babylonian mythology a complete explanation of its use. For as there are *watchers* mentioned also in the literature of the Parsees or Persian fire-worshippers, it has been argued that the Book of Daniel was a late book, which had borrowed its doctrines of angels from Zoroaster. Our enlarged knowledge of Babylonian literature has revealed to us the fact that they believed in a vast hierarchy of spiritual beings of every rank, some belonging to the earth and some to heaven; and among these the seven spirits, to whom the seven planets were entrusted, held an important place as the guardians of the universe and of the house. There were also seven warder spirits who kept guard at the gates of Hades. And each dwelling also had special watchers, whose office it was to drive away the wicked and all enemies, and who could even inflict upon them the penalty of death.

There have been brought home to our museums figures coarsely fashioned in bronze of these watchers; while in the cuneiform inscriptions there are found solemn forms, directing where, with magical rites, each one of these guardian beings was to be placed, and detailing his attributes and office. The being, therefore, which the king saw in his dream was one of his own guardians, a warder spirit under whose protection he had been placed. And we may probably, therefore, conclude that however severe might be the punishment, yet he would understand that it was intended for his good and not for his destruction. For it came from friends and not from foes.

The images of the king's dream naturally were taken from his own notions and ideas; but in verse 17 higher teaching was vouchsafed to him. He learned there something far better than his heathenish mythology; for that which he supposed to be by the decree of the watchers was really ordered to the intent that he might know that there is but one God Most High, and that He ruleth in the kingdom of men.

The decree was that the tree should be hewn down, its leaves shaken off, its fruit scattered; that no longer should the beasts find shelter beneath its shade, nor the birds lodge in its branches. Such words would have portended the total overthrow of Nebuchadnezzar and his dynasty, but for one remarkable reservation. The stump of the tree was not to be rooted up, but was to be bound tightly around with bands of iron and brass, and so was to remain wetted with the dews of heaven, and having its portion with the wild beasts in the grass of the earth.

In this there is mingled punishment and mercy. For if there was the hewing away of all beauty and grace, and the destruction of all strength and grandeur, yet was there hope in the guarded root. For those bands of brass and iron were for protection, and not for punishment. The king's mind would indeed be enwrapped in the darkness of a disturbed reason. Madness was to bind him fast. But these bands meant, not madness, but divine protection; for they were to secure the root from injury. At a time, and under circumstances when he could not protect himself, God would guard him from wrong. No foot might trample upon him; no hand of man might work his final extirpation.

But a strange destiny was in store. "Let his heart be changed from man's, and let a beast's heart be given unto him; and let seven times pass over him" (ver. 16).

The disease thus indicated is now generally acknowledged to have been a kind of madness called lycanthropy, because the person so afflicted, while retaining more or less his reason in other matters, supposes himself to be changed into some animal, whose conduct he imitates. The word lycanthropy properly applies only to those who supposed themselves changed into wolves, and who, under that idea, committed murders and hid themselves in dens away from mankind. Nebuchadnezzar seems to have supposed himself changed into an ox, or rather into one of those grand winged bulls which guarded the approaches to the palaces of the kings, and were symbols of the might and majesty of the gods. Even in his madness the fancies of the king take Babylonian forms, and are suggested to him by the sights with which he was daily conversant.

In his Lectures on Daniel, Dr. Pusey quotes an opinion of Dr. Browne, that Nebuchadnezzar throughout retained the sense of his personal identity, and was able to pray consciously to God. "I think it probable," he says, "because consistent with experience in similar forms of mental affection, that Nebuchadnezzar retained a perfect consciousness that he was Nebuchadnezzar during the whole course of his degradation, even while he ate 'grass as oxen;' and that he may have prayed fervently that the cup might pass from him."

For this he gives reasons. And if the king thus knew who and what he was, and could carry with him the remembrance of his past life, how strange must have been his thoughts, and how painful his experience during those "seven times!" A beast's heart had been given him, that is, an impulse from within forced him to act like an animal, to imitate its cries, to adopt its habits, to try to inhabit the same places, and feed upon the same kinds of nourishment; and yet all the while he knew that he was not an ox but a man. How distressing must have been the discord between the mania that had thus depraved one portion of his reason and the portion that was still sound! His great genius and mental ability were still there; for probably his intellectual gifts remained, clouded, indeed, but not destroyed; and yet he was forced to obey a diseased imagination, to forego his grandeur and all the cares of empire, nay, even to fall below the state and condition of a man, and adopt the life of a brute.

What Nebuchadnezzar suffered from was, therefore, a form of disease, rare indeed, but of which other well-authenticated instances have been recorded by medical men. And it is one of the many proofs of the credibility of the Book of Daniel, that we should thus find in it an account of a strange malady so described, as that the physical facts narrated agree with observations made since by scientific men in modern times. No author mentions this disease before the Christian era, and at first sight the whole narrative seems to belong to the region of the miraculous. But, as is so constantly the case in Holy Scripture, even miracles are in accordance with physical laws. The plagues of Egypt agree with phenomena natural in that country; and in the miracle recorded in Mark viii. 23–25, our Lord gave the blind man first the power of seeing; but all was confused, and men and trees were indistinguishable. The man plainly had not learned to use his eyesight, to measure distances, place things in their true relation, and correct the impression made upon the eye by the use of his reason. The images on the retina of the eye were right enough, but experience was wanting. Our Lord touched his eyes again, and gave in a moment that which the child acquires by years of observation. So here we have a species of mania now well known, but then absolutely new. And the description of it finds its explanation in facts since scientifically observed.

Even the assertion that Nebuchadnezzar prayed before his recovery, so marvellous in itself, is shown by similar cases, many of which are collected by Dr. Pusey, to be really an evidence of the reality of the facts recorded. We are not, however, to suppose that the king's reason was altogether unimpaired. It is said in verse 34 that "his understanding returned unto him," and though we are primarily to understand by this that the lycanthropic mania had departed, yet so terrible a disease must, to some extent, have obscured all the powers of his mind, though only partially. From time to time Nebuchadnezzar was able to reflect upon what he was and compare it with what he had been. And the dream and Daniel's interpretation had left their mark probably upon his memory. And so there was the knowledge that his humiliation was a punishment for pride. He had regarded himself as one whose power was supreme and irresistible. He now supposed himself to be an ox, with no other usefulness than to be a drudge and till the ground for man.

And thus the dream was "to the intent that the living might know that the Most High ruleth in the kingdom of men, and giveth it to whomsoever He will, and setteth up over it the lowest of men" (ver. 17).

It was a humiliating lesson for one so gifted, and raised to such greatness by a long course of victory in war and success in the arts of peace. When reciting the dream to Daniel, Nebuchadnezzar may have felt deep in his heart some incredulity. The kingdom of men had not, in his case, been given to a man of mean condition. But how would the words thrill through his memory when soon afterwards he deemed himself a mere animal, whose task was the plough. But all this was to come. At present he has only the dream, and summons Daniel to interpret it. It was the opening scene of a strange drama, but one sent for a moral purpose, to teach the king a great lesson, to humble his pride by a terrible punishment, and chiefly, as one may hope, to bring him to the footstool of Daniel's God in earnest repentance, and win for him a place among those rescued from eternal misery.

XII.

THE ASTONIED INTERPRETER.

(DANIEL iv. 19–27.)

WE have followed the king step by step in his recital of his dream to Daniel. We have seen how the imagery of it is taken from the sacred symbolism of the Assyrians, with whom the holy tree was the ordinary representative of majesty and power; and further, that the mental delusion which threatened to obscure the king's reason took its form from those colossal figures of winged bulls which adorned the walls of his palace and guarded its entrance. We have also seen that the description of the tree bears emphatic testimony to the energy of Nebuchadnezzar's rule, and the prosperity of the people subject to him. But the tree was to be hewn down, its branches cut off, its very leaves torn away, and its fruit scattered. And Daniel saw the dread meaning of this sentence, and sat "astonied for one hour, and his thoughts troubled him."

The word, however, rendered *hour* means only an indefinite time. Daniel sat astonied *for a while*. He had long served the king, and was probably attached to him personally; and this threatened overthrow of his rule was a grief to him. Probably Nebuchadnezzar, like Napoleon and other men of genius, exercised a fascination upon all brought into close contact with him; and besides this, what was to become of the kingdom when the strong arm was broken which had hitherto ruled it? Who was to take care of the throne during the seven years of the king's malady? A regency is often a disastrous thing now, with all our modern safeguards and systems of legal procedure. Power then resided in the will of one man, and when that will was enfeebled, murders and usurpations were the unfailing result. In this very case, within two years after Nebuchadnezzar's death, Babylon fell into a state of general anarchy. There was enough to trouble a good and wise man in the prospect of seven years of suspense; and especially as Daniel was himself the chief minister of state.

We may be sure that it was due to Daniel that those seven years passed over quietly, and that at the end of them Nebuchadnezzar once again peaceably occupied the throne. But as yet all was uncertain. Daniel saw the storm in front. He knew that the ship of the state would soon be sailing in troubled waters, assailed by many a gale of private faction, and beaten by many a tempest of popular commotion, of foreign attack, and of intrigue at home. He did not know that he would be able to guide the ship safely, and at the seven years' end restore to his master his kingly crown with its beauty and splendour undimmed.

"He sat astonied for a while," and Nebuchadnezzar saw the agitation of his feelings. As one anxious thought after another imprinted its mark upon Daniel's sorrowful countenance, the watching king felt that the dream boded him no good; but it is a proof of the generosity of his character that his trouble was not for himself, but for his faithful minister. Kindly and affectionately he bids him dispel his anxiety. "Let not the dream nor its interpretation trouble thee." And thus encouraged, Daniel broke silence, and said, "Would that the dream belonged to those who hate my lord, and its interpretation to his enemies."

Relieved by this sigh of anguish, he now repeats the king's description of the tree, amplifying its beauty and majesty, and pausing upon each particular of its greatness, as if unwilling to arrive at its conclusion. But at last it comes. The sacred tree is the symbol of the king, who in the years of his rule had grown strong and mighty, until his dominion—that is, his authority as a ruler—reached to the utmost end of his vast realm.

So far all was well. But the tree was to be hewn down, and this the prophet interpreted of the expulsion of Nebuchadnezzar, not only from his royal state, but from the use of his reason, and of his prerogatives as a man. For seven years he must be content to herd with the oxen, to deem himself one of their number, to try to eat their food, and live their life; rushing away from men, he was to make the forest or the marsh his home, and abandon all the comforts and refinements of human life.

But there was, first, a hope, and secondly, a purpose, in this chastisement. It was not to last for ever. There are trees which, when cut down, grow no more. The cedar, the cypress, the fir, throw up no suckers from their roots. But other trees may revive as long as the stump still exists in the ground (Job xiv. 7–9). The hewn down trunk of Jesse's race was to throw up a sucker that would attain to spiritual and eternal dominion (Isa. xi. 1). And here, after a period of obscurity, Nebuchadnezzar was once again to return to his royal glory. For his root was to be protected, " bound around with a band of iron and of brass," and its life was to be maintained by the gently falling dew of heaven.

It was, nevertheless, a sad hope; for it would be realised only after a long waiting. For seven years the king's reason would be clouded, his mind darkened by diseased imaginations, his palace occupied by others, his kingdom left to the care of strangers, and himself herding with the brutes. It was a terrible punishment. The loss of reason is the greatest affliction that can happen to any one; and here it was about to befall a man of extraordinary genius, who had mental gifts of the highest order, and who had cultivated and exercised these gifts, and who needed them for the government of the kingdom that he had built up.

And this terrible chastisement was no matter of chance. It had also a purpose. It was to last until the king knew and acknowledged that "there was one Most High, who ruleth in the kingdom of men, and giveth it to whomsoever He will."

"The Most High." There was something new to the king in this appellation. He had thought of many gods. The heavens were to him a repetition of the earth. There were beings there of every kind and class, good and evil, powerful for mischief, partial, capricious, but useful if propitiated. He thought that these beings existed for man's sake. He was to learn of one God, for and by whom all things exist, and who rules in the kingdom of men. He supposed that men such as himself, kings and princes, ruled, and that the gods would help or try to frustrate these earthly rulers according to the treatment which they themselves received. He had never conceived such a thought as that which is so natural to us, that while man proposes, God disposes of earthly things. Even the philosophical Greeks supposed that the Deity was subject to the rule of Necessity or Fate. Zeus might hold the balance, but the scale would go up or down independently of his will. But during these seven years there was to be a growth of knowledge in the king's mind, until he had mastered the truth that the earth is the Lord's, and that all things on earth are as He wills and His permission. Each man seems to b of action, a self-determining agent, one for himself, and acts as he chooses. And it is true that man, to a certain extent, can will and choose and act for himself. It is the dread gift his birthright: " Let us make a man in our image after our likeness, . . . and let him have dominion But this power does not exist apart from God. In all we will and do s willing and doing after His good pleasure. It is a deep mystery, this interlacing of the Divine and human will. But we feel quite sure that no power of any kind exists apart from God. It is His Omnipresence which endows all living things with activity. Even in things inanimate we know of no power except the presence of God. If a thing falls to the earth, if two things attract one another, we say it is by the law of gravitation. But there is no law without a lawmaker, no law apart from the active will of Him who maintains it in force; and the laws of nature are ordained by the wisdom and upheld by the energy of the will of God. The law of gravitation is God's ordering, its force is the presence of His will.

Nebuchadnezzar was to learn something of this. He was to learn that throned above the world was the Most High, and that He ruled in the kingdom of men. Whether they willed it or not, kings were His ministers, and their seeming freedom was to them, as it is to all men, because God has for wise reasons made the world a place of human probation. And we who see but our own one little world may repine, and wish that God had made it more pleasant, more easy, more safe, more free from trials and temptations and difficulties. If we could see all worlds, if we had perfect knowledge, and knew as also we are known, we should understand that our mental difficulties all arise from our

M

trying to judge where it is our duty and our privilege to obey. We have not the knowledge necessary for settling all speculative questionings, but only such practical guidance as may serve to direct us safely through the tangled maze of human life.

We are not told in what way Nebuchadnezzar was to attain to this humbling conviction. His malady may have been but partial, and many powers of his mind unimpaired; or there may have been lucid intervals from time to time, during which the king may have understood the intensity of his degradation, and also learned that better humiliation of sorrow for the sins which had brought him so low. Or it may have been only at the end of his seven years of lunacy when, with returning reason, there came an intense realisation of all that had happened; of his early grandeur and military renown; his success in the government of his vast realm; the glory of his buildings; the prosperity of his subjects; and, withal, of his pride, selfishness, cruelty, and of the arrogance and wilfulness of a despotic and irresistible tyranny. But whether the process was gradual, or whether there was but one cleansing in the burning furnace of concentrated self-accusation, and consciousness of the sins that had brought upon him the Divine wrath, the change in him was to be complete.

And the king's confession, when his reason finally came back, is that of a man on whom repentance has had its perfect work.

In verse 26 there is a very remarkable expression. Nebuchadnezzar's malady was to last until he had learned that "the heavens do rule." The idea cannot be that of the material heavens, which in some of the Assyrian hymns are regarded as "the father of the gods." For Daniel has been speaking of the Most High. It is one Supreme Being, a personal God, to whom he was endeavouring to raise the king's mind. But having clearly taught this unity and personality of the Deity, he now contents himself with a general expression of the great truth that power resides, not on earth, but above. It is not in this lower sphere that we are to look for the vital force which maintains sublunary things in order. Rather must we acknowledge, with St. James, that all things good, all gifts and endowments, all energies and powers, come down to us from above (James i. 17); and that this earth is but an emanation from heaven, called by God at first into existence, and still existing only as He wills, and as long as He wills. For " in God we live and move and have our being" (Acts xvii. 28); and apart from Him we are nothing.

Daniel, therefore, calls away the thoughts of the

king from earthly delusions to that Might enthroned above, which created the earth for the manifestation of the Divine glory, which has made man the object of heavenly love, and which still guides and regulates and sustains all earthly things. And that this Might is a personal being follows from Daniel's urgent remonstrance with the king. For the material heavens are indifferent to human conduct and human happiness. The sun shines as brightly upon the ruin of man's fortunes as upon his success. The advice given by Daniel implies the existence of a just Governor to whom the king is responsible for his deeds, and he bids him endeavour so to act as to incline this just Ruler of the world to be merciful unto him. "Wherefore, O king, let my counsel be acceptable unto thee, and break off thy sins by righteousness, and thine iniquities by showing mercy to the poor; if there may be a lengthening of thy tranquillity" (ver. 27).

Now we are not to suppose that this is mere general advice. Daniel was not likely at such a moment to give utterance to mere truisms, and say, Be a good man and all will go well. On the contrary, his words had direct reference to the king's previous conduct. Nebuchadnezzar had been a sagacious and successful ruler, but righteousness formed no part of his programme. His kingdom was built up by rapine and plunder. Habakkuk powerfully describes in chapter ii. the covetousness and lust of war and conquest that had marked the king's career. He had manifested no respect for the rights of others, but had been a scourge and flail for the beating down of all the nations far and near. And when he had overthrown their independent existence, he was not content with making them tributary, but dragged the unhappy people away, that, far from their homes, dispersed among strangers, they might be reduced to the condition of mere serfs, and live without hope or self-respect, deprived of all rights, and with no other safeguard for very existence than the will of a despotic conqueror.

And mercy was as entire a stranger from the heart of Nebuchadnezzar as was righteousness. The burden of Habakkuk's prophecy against the king is that chastisement must come "because of men's blood, and for the violence of the Chaldean land, and of the city of Babylon, and of all that dwell therein" (Hab. ii. 17). Nebuchadnezzar thought as little of human life as he did of the rights of nations and of justice. Those vast deportations of the inhabitants of a whole country must have been attended with an awful sacrifice of human lives. The path of those caravans must have been strewn with the corpses of all the sickly and the feeble among the people—with women that had been nurtured tenderly, and with young children left to die whenever their strength began to fail, and they could no longer keep pace with their captors on the march. Nor was Nebuchadnezzar's cruelty confined to these general schemes for the aggrandisement of the realm of the Chaldeans at the cost of so great human suffering and woe. For the pages of Holy Scripture set him before us as a fierce and brutal ruler, ready to butcher whole classes of men (Dan. ii. 12, 13), and delighting in modes of torture of a most savage description (ibid. iii. 19, 20; Jer. xxix. 22).

All this was to be changed. The king had been utterly unscrupulous in the carrying out of his designs, and not only foreign nations, but his own subjects and the exiles dwelling in his realms, had groaned under his stern despotism. Probably, too, in his vast buildings, he had used forced labour, as is, even now, too generally the case in Eastern lands, and thus every edifice would have cost vast numbers of human lives as well as terrible misery. It was as new a thought for Nebuchadnezzar that other people had rights, as that it was a God in heaven, and not himself on earth, that ruled in the affairs of men. Daniel's words may seem to us matters of course. As ages have passed by, men have learned that others have rights as well as themselves. And yet, even in our own century, we might find proof that a man of vast military genius may learn to use men merely as his instruments, and to think little, not merely of human misery in the abstract, but even of the lives and well-being of his own devoted followers.

It was, therefore, a very hard lesson which Nebuchadnezzar was called upon to learn. Every previous victory, every success in war, every exercise in past time of his despotic powers, had tended to make him arrogant, selfish, wilful, incapable of self-restraint, indifferent to the wishes and happiness of others. Terrible was to be his punishment. For seven years he was to account himself a brute, and spend his life with the beasts. But when reason returned there were to come with it better things. There were to come self-restraint, respect for the rights of men, mercy even for the erring. Daniel's words, it may be, ate into the king's heart like burning fire. During his humiliation, often and again they may have sounded in his ears like some strain of music which comes unbidden. Righteousness — he had never practised it or troubled about it before. Mercy — never before had he shown himself gentle or forgiving. It was a great change, to be wrought by an extraordinary intervention of God's Providence. And if Nebuchadnezzar throughout his history stands forth as a remarkable man, in himself not unworthy of the Divine dealings with him; if, too, his history indicates to us that the Gentiles were the object of the Divine regard, and not the Jews only, yet the lesson is for general use and for the teaching of all mankind. Only we mercifully can learn our lesson by the example of others, and gather instruction for our lives and conduct by narratives such as this. For in the pages of the Bible the veil is partially removed, and we see God's ways with men clearly set forth, and learn what are His purposes, not only in the rising and fall of kingdoms, but even more in the prosperity and the chastisement of the men whose acts and lives are there set forth before us. We may never have had the power to sin on so grand a scale as Nebuchadnezzar did, nor have to bear so strange a punishment. But we all may meet with merited chastisement, and well will it be for us if we meditate upon its purpose, and with humble penitence break off from our sins and seek for healing and restoration from One, no longer revealed to us as the "Most High," but as our Father in heaven, reconciled to us by the blood of His dear Son.

XIII.

THE ROYAL PENITENT.

(DANIEL iv. 28-37.)

"ALL this came upon the king Nebuchadnezzar" (ver. 28). Strange must it seem that a vision so remarkable as that of the sacred tree, and of the watcher ordering it to be hewn down, and the dread menace of years of lunacy, should have produced no change in the king's ways. Naturally, it seems to us that if we had been in Nebuchadnezzar's place, and had known so clearly that a great retribution was hanging over our heads, we should have ceased not day or night to pray God that He would withdraw His chastising hand. And Daniel had even urged this upon the king's mind, and tried to lead him to the hope of a lengthened tranquillity, to which he could attain only by true penitence and the breaking away from the paths of sin.

Yet, really, Nebuchadnezzar acted as the majority of men act now. They do not doubt that their sins will find them out, and, nevertheless, they go on in the same dull course, putting away all thought of consequences, not by any forcible act, but by simply contenting themselves with their daily habitual course of life. Day by day they discharge their ordinary duties, become victims of their usual temptations, give way to the same self-indulgences, and never really reflect upon the issues of their conduct. Then perhaps sickness comes, and they have quiet, thoughtful times, and see death close at hand; or some sorrow or misfortune overtakes them, and in their depression serious misgivings force themselves upon their minds, and good resolutions are made, and it seems as if a sinner were rescued from ruin. But time, with its soft hand, heals the sorrow, and health takes the place of sickness; and once again we are surrounded by the din of constant occupation, and our old ways resume their wonted mastery. In our hours of sickness or grief we were, for the time, rescued from the strong current that was hurrying us along in its rapid course. Withdrawn from its force, we were lifted up, as it were, for a while, and placed upon the river's bank, that we might reflect upon the direction which the stream of our life was taking, and ask ourselves—What will the end be? Whither hasten we so lightly and so fast? But gradually the current draws us in again, and we are borne along as carelessly as before.

Now we should lose the benefit of our Bible lessons if we supposed that the more evident presence of the supernatural made the probation of those of whom we there read different in kind from our own. God reveals Himself now, by the voice of conscience, quite as clearly as He then manifested His presence by miracle or prophecy. Many a sinner, under the influence of sermon or prayer, or the reading of Holy Scripture, is as fully convinced of God's care for him, and that a call has reached him " to break off his sins by righteousness," as Nebuchadnezzar could have been. The sin of Iscariot may have been of deeper dye than that of Caiaphas, because he had had greater opportunities of hearing our Lord's words and witnessing His mighty acts. But in itself the sin of both was identical. Both for private ends put away from them the conviction that Jesus of Nazareth was their Messiah, and both for worldly gains joined in compassing His death. And men commit the same sin now, when they put to silence the inner voice which tells them that Christ is the Saviour of sinners. Nebuchadnezzar here did what every sinner does who has ever felt conviction of sin, and has let the emotion pass away unused. And so punishment took its course. He might have so used the warning as to have escaped it. For a time, possibly, he was deeply affected; but day by day the remembrance of the dream and of its interpretation withdrew into the background. He was fully occupied with the affairs of his kingdom, had to attend to his army, to his buildings, to the great works for bridling the course of the Euphrates, and to the thousand and one cares of state. Each day couriers came with tidings of importance, and the king neglected none of them. The one thing he did neglect was himself. He had had warning, but he let other things hide it away.

And God was long-suffering. Month after month passed, each bringing its opportunity. The balance is still held even. The uplifted hand forbears the blow. Would Nebuchadnezzar recall the warning to mind, or let it quite pass away? God does not hurry the decision, but waits; and when the choice was fully made then the punishment came.

"At the end of twelve months he walked in the palace of the kingdom of Babylon. The king spake, and said, Is not this great Babylon, that I have built for the house of the kingdom by the might of my power, and for the honour of my majesty?" He has had a whole year's respite, and at the end of the time is as selfish and arrogant as ever. All thought of the depth of degradation that is before him has slipped away from his mind. We seem to see him as he paces to and fro on the flat roof of the vast palace that he has built. His great officers of state are in attendance, and follow him reverently, and as he reaches the end of the terrace and turns round, they stand aside that he may pass through; and then respectfully follow him again. But he marks not their presence. His whole mind is taken up with pride and vainglory at what he has done. There still remains a solid mass of masonry towering above the ruins of the royal palace, and on this probably Nebuchadnezzar was walking. Stretched on all sides below him was "Babylon the great," and though the city was really of vast antiquity, yet he had so added to it, had so strengthened and beautified it, that he might fairly claim it as his work. He had constructed those mighty walls, which long remained the wonder of the world. He had dug the course for the Euphrates, building massive barriers of brick on each side to confine its waters, with flights of steps and gates of brass to lead down to it. Many of his wars had been waged that he might force the conquered people to come and inhabit its vacant spaces. Within he had reared temples and observatories, and hanging gardens for the pleasure of his wife, and palaces for royal abode. Myriads torn from their homes were toiling below. He thought not of their heavy hearts, their ruined homes, their hopeless misery. His one thought was that all he saw was for his own gratification. It was a wonderful work that lay around him, and he had been the doer of it. His empire was the foremost of earthly realms, and he was its founder. Never was a man more thoroughly the author of his own greatness than Nebuchadnezzar. To his own genius, his own military prowess, his own powers of statesmanship he owed everything. He had achieved all " by the might of his own power, and for the honour of his own majesty." Self was uppermost in his mind. There was no thought of the purpose for which God had so exalted him; no thought of God whatsoever; and no thought of man except as his slave, and the mean creature who must do as he willed. Never was pride and arrogance more inflated; and never was humiliating punishment more near.

For " while the word was in the king's mouth, there fell a voice from heaven, saying, O King Nebuchadnezzar, to thee it is spoken; the kingdom is departed from thee. And they shall drive thee from men, and thy dwelling shall be with the beasts of the field; they shall make thee to eat grass as oxen, and seven times shall pass over thee, until thou know that the Most High ruleth in the kingdom of men, and giveth it to whomsoever He will."

This was the lesson which the king had to learn (ver. 25), and he might have learned it joyfully in peace. The appeal had been made to his conscience. He had been warned by a wonderful dream, and Daniel had shown him what was the Divine purpose. But twelve months had passed away, and the lesson was still unlearned; and now he must be taught it after a sterner fashion. And to us also is it spoken: for God's dealings with mankind are the same yesterday, to-day, and for ever. We have to learn also the lesson of God's rule, and that we are responsible to Him for all our thoughts and words and deeds. But ill would it be for us if God taught us in only one manner. There is a manifold diversity in the ways of His Providence, though the purpose is ever the same. He calls us by His mercies and His love; by the voice of conscience within, and by the varied events which meet us in our pathway through the world. He has surrounded us with diverse means of Grace, both special and ordinary; and sometimes, it may be, extraordinary occurrences waken us from our apathy, and summon us to repentance. Happy are those who listen to the still, small voice, and grasp the loving hand stretched forth in mercy. For God has also terrors, and strokes of affliction hard and grievous to be borne, and the rod of the impenitent falls upon them in the sharpness of punishment. It was this smiting rod which Nebuchadnezzar must suffer, because he had hardened himself against all gentler means.

"A voice fell from heaven." Whether this voice reached only the heart of the king, or whether a sound as of thunder reverberated through the air, we know not. But at once the words of warning, which he had so long forgotten, came back to his mind. What force of terror in those words, "To thee it is spoken." To his officers of state there was a sudden noise. It passed away, and had for them no meaning. "To me it is spoken." Again and again this pealed in the king's ears. And as his courtiers watched they saw a strange change pass over him. A minute before he had stood there, haughty, arrogant, in the full consciousness of his power, his supremacy, his mighty genius. His eye was clear, his gaze steady, his actions self-controlled. Now all is unsteady; the eye wanders, the look is furtive and downcast. The mind no longer rules his actions; reason has been dethroned, and strange delusions have taken its place. He is no longer the king, the sovereign master of all around. He fancies himself to be an ox, and with a cry of loud despair rushes away, that he may hide himself in the deep thickets. For the punishment that had been withheld so long as there was possibility of repentance has now come suddenly.

"The same hour was the thing fulfilled upon Nebuchadnezzar: and he was driven from men, and he did eat grass as oxen, and his body was wet with the dew of heaven, till his hairs were grown like eagles' feathers, and his nails like birds' claws."

How complete and terrible was this retribution! Madness in all cases is a most sad form of disease, and not unfrequently it befalls men of distinguished genius. Often there seems but a narrow dividing line between some of the noblest gifts of intellect and imaginations that overpower the reason, and soar into ungoverned and disordered heights. Possibly Nebuchadnezzar had long given way to excited dreams of conquest, and of his great city becoming the centre of the world, and of his throne being the seat of all earthly dominion; and now all is changed. He supposes himself to be a wild animal, and is driven from men, not by their act though there was little pity for the insane in those days, but by his own fears and illusions. And seven years pass over him, during which he wanders in the forests, feeding on such food as they produced, and each day becoming more like the wild beasts who found there their proper home.

We can quite believe that during this time he was not left without anxious care and attendance. His restoration to his kingdom immediately that he was healed of his disease proves that there were those who maintained for him his rights. His wife Amytis, for whose happiness he had done so much, Daniel, his faithful vizier, would neither of them neglect him; and so, while he supposed himself to be an ox, they may have supplied him with needful food, and encouraged him to remain in some sheltered thicket, where they could take care of him, could guard him from molestation, and do all that was possible for his health and comfort.

" And at the end of the days I Nebuchadnezzar lifted up mine eyes unto heaven, and mine understanding returned unto me, and I blessed the Most High, and I praised and honoured Him that liveth for ever, whose dominion is an everlasting dominion, and His kingdom is from generation to generation; and all the inhabitants of the earth are reputed as nothing; and He doeth according to His will in the army of heaven, and among the inhabitants of the earth: and none can stay His hand, or say unto Him, What doest Thou?"

We have already seen that it is an observed fact in cases of lycanthropy, that there are sane intervals when the sufferer is conscious of his state, and when there is a strong inclination to prayer and to religious emotion. In this case, moreover, the allotted period of punishment was at an end, and as it had been preceded by arrogance and self-laudation, so the return to sanity begins in humiliation and prayer. It is possible, and even probable, that the king had had several such periods of self-consciousness, when, hidden away in some leafy recess, he had reflected upon his past life and the strange punishment which had overtaken him. And in them God's grace had wrought in him that abiding change which made him willing to humble himself by publishing this decree, in which he frankly acknowledged both his sin and the punishment which it had brought upon him. And now it had done its work, and taught him the lesson which he might have learned less painfully, that God is supreme, and that man must obey Him and work for Him. But how often is it with us that we bring upon ourselves severe chastisement because we are so deaf to God's voice when He speaks to us gently. Yet happy was Nebuchadnezzar that at last conviction had been wrought in him; for not always does chastisement produce its intended purpose. There are those who harden themselves against God's anger as erewhile they had done against His love. And what more can He do for His people? He tries to win them by love, and they give themselves to riot and vanity; He visits them with the scourge, and they rebel and defy Him.

It was not so here, and therefore the last days of Nebuchadnezzar were days of peace and tranquillity. "At the same time my reason returned unto me; and for the glory of my kingdom, mine honour and brightness returned unto me; and my counsellors and my lords sought unto me; and I was established in my kingdom, and excellent majesty was added unto me."

His chastisement was at an end. No traces of it were to remain, but the rest of his days were to be spent in undimmed splendour. Besides the honour and dignity of his royal state, the brightness of his countenance was restored to him. Once again there was the clear eye, the expressive look, the face full of meaning. There was no furtive glance, no clouded, wandering avoidance of the look of others, no dazed, uncertain mien, but the dignity of right reason, and the voice giving utterance to wise thought and calm resolve. It is remarkable that he did not of himself return to seek again his throne. Probably his frightful personal appearance, with his hair long and matted together, and his nails like claws, made him ashamed. Probably, too, there was faith. His punishment had come literally as God had spoken, and equally certain of fulfilment was the promise of restoration.

But how was it that his lords thus came to seek him? It must have been Daniel's doing, and probably he had been the wise counsellor who had kept the affairs of state in good order, and the throne open for the king's return, during the seven years of banishment. In so new a kingdom there were dangerous forces at work for its ruin. Evil-Merodach, the son of Nebuchadnezzar, reigned scarcely three years, and was then murdered, to make room for a succession of men who usurped the crown by violence. It is a grand tribute to Nebuchadnezzar as a ruler that for seven years his subjects waited for him, and that no conspiracy or intrigue closed against him the return to empire. But there must have been a wise regent during his absence, or things would have fallen to pieces of themselves. States subjected against their will would have rebelled; wild tribes, freed from stern control, would have carried rapine and desolation far and wide; quarrels among the great nobles would have led to partisan contests; and oppression unchecked would have ended in violent commotions. Whoever was regent was a wise, an energetic, a just, and an unselfish ruler; and that regent apparently was Daniel. Even if the queen, Amytis, nominally held the office, yet Daniel would be her minister, and in chapter v. 11 we have proof of the high estimation in which he was held by the royal house.

And Daniel too would know when the appointed years of punishment were over. He had waited for the time when once again he could bring back his master to the throne. Alike faithful to his king and his God, he had borne the great weight of those seven years of care and anxiety in the sure confidence that the word of God was true, and that the root had been bound about with iron and brass in order that out of it might again spring the mighty tree of royal grandeur.

And as the seven years drew near their end, both the queen and the vizier would redouble their care. Probably during his mania Nebuchadnezzar had fled away from all human approach. Certain things they could do for him, but the chief thing was to guard his haunt from being visited by any but themselves, and by themselves even in such a way as not to alarm him. But now the set time had come, and they summon his lords, and go forth to find him in the wood where he usually wandered. And doubtless there were many who ridiculed their expedition, many more who doubted. The queen, they would say, had held the reins of power upon the plea that Nebuchadnezzar was alive. Was he really so? Should they find him at all? If so, in what state? If still a lunatic, what should they do with him? If they brought him back with long unkempt hair and nails, and lowing like an ox, would the Chaldeans obey him? or consent any longer to endure a woman's rule, when they saw what was the condition of the being in whose name she governed? Strange thoughts must have filled their minds as they went forth to hunt the woods for the maniac, who seven years ago had rushed away from all human converse to herd with the beasts.

But under Daniel's influence they went; and they found a man strange in his outward aspect, but waiting for their coming, sure that they would come; and so serene and bright in look, so wise in words, so dignified in mien, that they reverently bent the knee before him, and acknowledged him for their king. And he bent before God, and published his decree of humiliation, and, withal, of praise and thanksgiving. "Now I Nebuchadnezzar praise, and extol, and honour the King of heaven, all whose works are truth, and His ways judgment; and those that walk in pride He is able to abase."

XIV.

BELSHAZZAR THE KING.

(Daniel v. 1-4.)

WE are living in an age when knowledge is so wonderfully multiplied that scarcely is the ink of one statement dry before fresh records are discovered, giving us certainty where before we had conjecture only. And in almost every case this increased knowledge removes difficulties which sceptics had previously used for throwing doubt upon the accuracy of the Biblical record. They had made merry over the kingdom of the Hittites, so often mentioned in the earlier books of Holy Scripture. That kingdom has now come to light, and in the Egyptian records we find ample proof of its grandeur, and that the Hittites were a learned and civilised people, and so powerful that they contended on equal terms with the Pharaohs for supremacy in Western Asia. Equal ridicule was cast upon Elam, as if it were an invention of the prophets. The cuneiform inscriptions confirm the accuracy of the prophetic declarations, by showing that Cyrus was actually king of Elam, and that Elam and Media were the conquerors of Babylon (Isaiah xxi. 2). So here Belshazzar seemed to give a great triumph to the sceptic, who boldly asserted that there was no such king, and behold, now his history is gradually coming to light. The preservation of these old records is a striking instance of the Divine Providence. In Egypt the climate is so dry that even manuscripts remain for centuries as bright and clear as when first written. But ordinary writing materials would quickly have perished in Assyria and Babylonia. And there the people inscribed their records on clay, and only rarely on paper or parchment. Cumbrous as it may seem, clay was really a cheap and convenient material, and tiles made of it and carefully dried or burnt were practically imperishable. We possess no Greek manuscript earlier than the third century after Christ, unless it be that lately discovered at Constantinople by Archbishop Bryennios, containing "The Teaching of our Lord by the Twelve Apostles." This is far older than any other known Greek writing; but we have in the British Museum inscribed clay tablets certainly as ancient as the time of Abraham.

Now the difficulty about Belshazzar was this: the Babylonian empire survived the death of Nebuchadnezzar for scarcely a quarter of a century, and during that period profane history gives us the record of only four kings, Evil-Merodach, Neriglissar, Laborosoarchad, and Nabonidus. It relates, moreover, the fall of Nabonidus, also called Labynetus, in such a way as to prove that he was not Belshazzar. For after being defeated in the open field, it describes him as throwing himself into the strong fortress of Borsippa, where he maintained his defence until some time after the fall of Babylon, but finally capitulated to Cyrus, who spared his life and sent him into Carmania, where Abydenus says, but untruly, that he even became satrap. Within the last few years the cuneiform inscriptions have made it certain that Belshazzar not only existed, but that he was neither Evil-Merodach, as some have supposed, nor identical with Nabonidus, according to the arguments of others. Cylinders of Nabonidus have been found in which he prays for "Belshazzar (spelt Bel-sarusar), his eldest son, the offspring of his heart." And quite recently Mr. Rassam has discovered cylinders, which have been translated for us by Sir H. Rawlinson and Mr. Pinches, throwing great light upon the fall of Babylon, and of which Mr. Sayce has given us a popular account in "Fresh Light from the Ancient Monuments" (pp. 166–183).

In one of these, in which Nabonidus describes his restoration of various temples, repeated mention is made of "the king's son," as evidently a person of much importance; and it is very probable that Nabonidus, who was not of royal descent, had married a daughter of Nebuchadnezzar, who thus would be father or grandfather of Belshazzar, as described in verses 2 and 11. With this virtually agrees the statement of Herodotus that there was a Labynetus, son of Labynetus and Nitocris, a Babylonian queen. The mistake is simply that of confusing the son with the father. Now, whether Belshazzar ever bore his father's name is unknown to us; and though quite possible, yet it is more probable that Herodotus, who wrote at a distance, confused the stories which he heard. But the importance attached to Nitocris in his history confirms our belief that she was a daughter of Nebuchadnezzar. According to Herodotus Labynetus (Nabonidus) was a successful ruler, and the builder of stately palaces and temples. The cylinders agree with this. Among other temples they especially mention his restoration of those at Haran and Sepharvaim; and they show that in the earlier part of his reign he even defeated Cyrus, and took Astyages prisoner, though doomed subsequently to fall beneath their attack. Herodotus had but a very general idea of Babylonian history, and knew nothing even of Nebuchadnezzar.

We now know that the son of Nabonidus was associated with his father in the government; and one cylinder gives the name of the last king of Babylon as Merodachsarusar, wherein the name of Merodach seems substituted for that of Bel. As Belshazzar did nothing worth recording, and died ingloriously before his father, we could not expect more than these incidental references to him. But two of the cylinders discovered by Mr. Rassam detail the history of the capture of Babylon. Cyrus appears in them as a Persian by descent, but as actual king of Elam, and his success is represented as chiefly owing to the disaffection of Nabonidus' own subjects. As the result it is expressly said that he "entered Babylon without fighting," not by any such method as Herodotus describes, but apparently by treachery. Such a banquet as that given by Belshazzar would evidently offer a favourable opportunity for the city's betrayal. Nabonidus is described as endeavouring in vain to resist the advance of the Elamite army under Gobryas, the general of Cyrus, and as having fled away when Sippara opened its gates to the invaders without any attempt at defence. Some time after the surrender of Babylon Cyrus captures Nabonidus, and puts him in fetters, and at some subsequent time " the king dies." Mr. Sayce by the king understands Nabonidus, but Mr. Deane, in Bishop Ellicott's Commentary, supposes that it was Belshazzar, and that, as a great mourning is immediately described as having taken place for him at Accad, the scene of the events recorded in this chapter was not Babylon but Accad. But as Nabonidus is mentioned by name in the previous line, and as he was the supreme king, it is plain that he must be the person meant, and the public mourning for him at Accad, and the honourable burial accorded him by Cambyses, the son of Cyrus, "in the temple of the Sceptre of the World," confirm the accounts given by the Greek historians of the merciful treatment he met with from Cyrus, even though at his first capture he was thrown into fetters; and his death apparently was not by violence, but from natural causes.

To sum then this matter up, these two cylinders which give us the account from Cyrus's side of his conquest of the Chaldean empire, and his capture of Babylon, show that Nabonidus made a brave defence in the open field, and that he fell owing to the disaffection of his subjects. They set Cyrus before us as fomenting this disaffection, which prevailed even among the Chaldeans, and would be more general among those nations which, like the Jews, had been torn from their own countries to dwell as strangers in the waste parts of the dominions of Nebuchadnezzar. As Babylon especially had a large proportion of foreigners among its inhabitants, it is not surprising that like Sippara it surrendered itself to Cyrus without resistance ; and if the Jews aided in this surrender, we have an additional reason for the conqueror's kindness to them, and for his restoration of them to their land. There does not seem to be in these two cylinders any direct reference to Belshazzar. Apparently he was a dissolute prince, and was content to trust in the strong walls of Babylon while his father was making outside a vain but courageous defence. But there were enemies within the city ; and encouraged by the defeat of Nabonidus, the malcontents made their own terms with Cyrus, who, when admitted within the walls, treated them kindly and granted them peace. Probably while the banquet was going on the conspirators were gathering noiselessly round the youthful king, and put him to death before surrendering the city to the invaders. And having made no defence, and falling thus ingloriously, there was nothing either in his life or death which merited mention at the hand of the chronicler of Cyrus's victories. Of Nabonidus it is expressly said that his capture was subsequent to the peaceful entry of Cyrus into Babylon.

Fresh documents will probably be found which will give us fuller information of the fall of Babylon. Meanwhile, these tablets of clay have given us contemporaneous proof that Nabonidus, Babylon's last king, had a son, named Bel-sarusar; that as "the king's son" he held a place of high authority; that Babylon fell without resistance; and that Nabonidus was not at Babylon when it surrendered itself to Cyrus. Bearing these facts in mind, we may now consider the inspired history.

It tells us, then, that Belshazzar, recking little of the enemy outside the walls, made a great feast. While his father was fighting for the throne, this youthful voluptuary gathers his nobles together for feasting. Secure within the massive walls of Babylon he cares little for the war raging without. For fourteen years Cyrus had been subjugating to his rule the vast regions which extend from the Euxine to the Persian Gulf, and he was now gathering his forces for the final campaign which was to make him the head of the second universal monarchy. Daniel, no doubt, when he entered the royal presence, and said, " God hath numbered thy kingdom and finished it," bore in mind Nebuchadnezzar's dream of the image whose " brightness was excellent, and its form terrible," but had any record of it been preserved in the royal house? Had they handed down any tradition even that Babylon, the head of gold, was to give place to a second universal monarchy, the breadth of whose dominions was typified by the breast of silver, and the two nations who shared the sovereignty by the wide-reaching arms? Probably we all only too readily forget warnings that are disagreeable to us, and Belshazzar, still surrounded by all the pomp and magnificence of an Oriental court, thought little of the dangers gathering round him, and full of confidence in the impregnable fortifications of his vast city, was too unobservant to discern, or try to remove, the discontent and ill-will that would so soon make the defenders of the brazen gates throw them open to the invader without an effort at defence.

Still we must not rate Belshazzar too meanly. If Nabonidus married Nitocris immediately upon his coming to the crown, Belshazzar would have been about fourteen years of age when he was first associated with his father in the government (cf.

o

chap. viii. 1). Surrounded by wise counsellors, and with the aid of his mother, Nitocris, he would not be too young for the office, especially in a climate where both mind and body develop more rapidly than in our colder regions. And evidently his father thought him quite capable of managing the internal affairs of the kingdom while he chose a soldier's life. For two years Nabonidus withstood the advance of the Elamite army, but even after his resistance had failed, and he was shut up in Borsippa, Belshazzar, now called to act as sole king, still made head against the invaders. There was evidently some vigour in his character, joined with voluptuousness, and but for treachery he might have foiled all Cyrus's attacks. Perhaps it was after some partial success that he made this banquet and " drank wine before the thousand."

This was in accordance with Oriental practice. The drinking began after the feast was over, and the king, seated at a separate table in front of his guests, set them the example of dissolute indulgence.

And as the wine mastered his better sense, " Belshazzar, whiles he tasted the wine, commanded to bring the golden and silver vessels which his father Nebuchadnezzar had taken out of the temple which was in Jerusalem; that the king, and his princes, his wives, and his concubines, might drink therein."

Now this act may very probably have been suggested to Belshazzar by the known disaffection of the Jews. There can be little doubt that they shared fully in that dislike to the government of Nabonidus to which Cyrus ascribes the comparative ease of his conquest of Babylonia. After Sippara had thrown open its gates to Gobryas, and Nabonidus had found himself unable to maintain his defence, the revolt of the whole country would rapidly follow; and though kept down by force at Babylon, Belshazzar, of course, knew that the Jews were among the most zealous of the friends of Cyrus, and when the wine began to inflame him it was an easy advance to insult and bravado. The phrase "tasting the wine" does not imply moderate drinking. As the entertainer, Belshazzar took the first sip of the wine provided for the banqueters, and then the carouse began. And as probably he sat down full of anger against the Jews, whose strong feelings of patriotism and their exclusive religion always made them stand apart from all heathen nations, there is nothing incredible in his thus commanding the holy vessels to be brought forth, though for seventy years they had remained unmoved in the temples, where they had been the objects of constant attention as a splendid prize of war. Now there they had been regarded as holy; offered to Bel as a trophy of victory over the God of Jerusalem, they had been kept sacred, and applied to no profane use. But Belshazzar determines now to put them to unholy employment. Those Jews, so firm in their love to their country, so faithful to their God, forming a race so alien and separate and self-contained among the motley dwellers at Babylon, shall see their God disgraced, and the vessels which they regard with such heartfelt veneration shall be desecrated. The command is given, and it is done. "The golden vessels taken out of the temple of the house of Elohim at Jerusalem are brought forth; and the king, and his princes, his wives, and his concubines, drank in them."

The profanity added zest to the carousal. "They drank wine, and praised the gods of gold, and of silver, of brass, of iron, of wood, and of stone."

There is a grim severity in this long enumeration. They had gods of every conceivable material, but material gods only. They had gods of every sort; of gold and silver for the rich; of brass and iron for the middle classes; of wood and stone for the poor. But in one respect they were all alike. All were powerless; they had no breath in them.

There was, then, in this banquet, not voluptuousness only, but profanity. It had begun in sensuousness, and as with each draught of wine the flesh waxed more wanton, all better and reverent thought, and all sense of decency passed away. It made their pleasure more intense when in their enjoyment they could make poor jests about the God who claimed to be the One God, the sole Ruler of heaven and earth. And, as history so often witnesses, the intemperate revel, the coarse mockery, were but the precursors of sudden punishment. Wherever profanity and wantonness meet, it needs no inspired eye to see the hand writing its condemnation upon the wall. The eye of every thoughtful person can see it. Every mind taught by the examples of the past trembles at the thought of the sure nearness of retribution. Above all must one who believes in the rule of a just God feel that such conduct must certainly be visited. Here it was visited; and we shall quickly see the wonderful manner of the Divine retribution.

XV.

THE HANDWRITING ON THE WALL.

(DANIEL v. 5-9.)

WE have but lately read the history of Belshazzar's sacrilege. Close upon its commission came retribution. The festival that was to mock the God of Israel, and proclaim the triumph of man over Him who made heaven and earth, ends in man's discomfiture. The thousand lords cannot save their master. They had come to share in his impiety, and be witnesses of his bold effrontery. They see him pale and agitated; his knees smite one against another. All his strength has vanished; his pride is humbled. They behold in him a culprit on whom sentence is being passed. He is weighed before them and found wanting, and his kingdom is taken from him, and given to his adversaries.

The very banquet that was to celebrate his triumph had aided in his downfall. Trusting to the mighty walls which his grandfather had built, he forgot that the empire won by force must be consolidated by justice, and that ramparts of brick could avail nothing against discontent and disaffection rankling within. And that very temper which could delight in this festival, prepared for the set purpose of showing therein his arrogance, and for using words of boasting over a conquered people, is just the temper that urges even the weakest to resistance, and by the sharpness of its sting incites to stern reprisals.

Babylon was peopled by races torn from their native lands. With a powerful enemy outside the walls, these transplanted nations would naturally be restless and eager to throw off the yoke. Perhaps none were more restless than the Jews. A nation which can look back upon a noble history is always high-spirited. The men whose memories were stored with the exploits of Moses and Joshua, of Gideon, and Barak, and David: nay, who in their great heroes recognised men raised up by their God, and filled with His Spirit; such men would be ever on the look-out for the appearance among them of a new heaven-sent leader, and the remembrance of Jeremiah's prophecy of the seventy years would help to keep their minds high strung, and their hearts beating with expectation. How could such a race be ought else than restless and unquiet?

And the king at such a crisis insults them! And he does so in that possession which all earnest men will never endure to see insulted—in their religion. A man will bear much himself, but he will not bear insult to his wife and children. And those even who have borne the violation of their domestic rights have risen in anger at sacrilege. The Israelites had probably borne of late many wrongs at Babylon. There had been years of anarchy, when the weak have always much to suffer; and Daniel, who had been their powerful protector in the days of Nebuchadnezzar, had long been living in retirement, while others were at the head of affairs. When the king gave orders to bring forth and profane their sacred vessels, we may feel sure that this was no isolated act. Other wrongs and insults had gone before. It was no mere sudden ebullition of drunken folly. The Jews were suspected by him and disliked, and he had made them feel his anger. There is no reason to doubt the truth of Cyrus's assertion, that the empire of Babylon fell, not through his valour and skilfulness in war, but because of the disaffection of its own subjects. We can scarcely be wrong in considering that the Jews were fully as disaffected as any of the other motley tribes who had been brought against their will to Babylon; and Belshazzar no doubt knew that they were among the many who were hoping for his downfall; and he hated them for it. And to make them feel his displeasure he will remind them that they are a conquered race. He will gather round him his Chaldean lords, and will bring forth their sacred vessels and put them to unholy use. The act will bring back to memory that the house of their God lies desolate and in ruins. Nay, more. He will treat their God as one that has quite passed away, and their temple as a forgotten thing. For the vessels hitherto carefully preserved shall be put to common use, as things no longer worth any special notice or regard. Alike the God and the place to which they belonged may now be considered as blotted out of mind. Such an insult would sting them to the quick, and rouse even the most timid to bitter vengeance. And with angry feelings all around, and men gnashing their teeth in indignation, the king calls away his officers from their posts, that they may spend the night in revelry.

Among those thousand lords must have been most of the men high in rank, and competent to see that the king's matters suffered no damage; men whose keen eyes would have detected gathering mischief, and whose very presence would have kept the disaffected in awe. He bids them leave their various duties, that their attendance at the banquet may give point to an insult, and make its barbs more irritating.

Such acts add nothing to a ruler's strength. Even those who take part in them secretly disapprove, and lose their confidence in the wisdom of their chief. And meanwhile the disaffected were left free to carry out their own plans. The carouse would give them the very opportunity they wanted. When the king and a thousand of his officers were indulging in the revel, it is not probable that sober watch and careful discipline would be maintained elsewhere.

The thoughtful at such times need no handwriting upon the wall to tell them that punishment is near. The pages of profane history are full of narratives which show that a night of revelry is constantly the precursor of the day of doom, and that "vengeance as a lion lieth in wait for those that mock" (Ecclus. xxvii. 28). But one great use of Holy Scripture is that it shows us God's presence openly manifested in His dealings with human affairs. His hand is ever really present at all times, working in the events of this world, but it is wrapped about with clouds. Still no one can read history with care and not find the same lesson that is taught by Belshazzar's feast. The lives of

Philip II. of Spain, of Louis XIV. of France, and of Napoleon, all teach it, as do those of myriads of meaner men; only God punished their pride and ambition by the sure though silent working of His ordinary laws, while here He gave a sign which clearly indicated that those laws are the ministers of His unchanging justice.

And so the handwriting upon the wall has passed into a proverb, and wherever we see pride and want of self-control, we know that punishment is near; and in the self-willed acts which mark the climax of a presumptuous course, we see the handwriting which tells us that the man has reached the edge of the precipice, and that his next step will be utter ruin. And this principle is true in ordinary life, and in the fortunes of institutions quite as much as in that of despots, and conquerors, and statesmen. It is an old saying of the poet Hesiod that "the half is more than the whole," because by moderation and self-restraint we may keep the half, while we shall gain the whole only to see it wrested from us. The papacy overthrew not only itself, but strangled Christianity in those realms where its influence was chief, by attaining to despotic power over the very consciences of men. Were any one form of Church government able to crush out all its rivals in England, it would thereby ensure its own ruin. Were one political party able to silence the rest, it would only fall thereby into more utter powerlessness. And so in the management of our own lives, our gifts become our bane instead of being our blessing, when we cannot control ourselves. We have the principle set before us in the life of the most active and highly gifted of the apostles. For at the very time when more than ordinary revelations were made to St. Paul, and he was even caught up into the third heaven, and heard things beyond the power of human language to utter, God at that very time placed a thorn in his flesh to buffet him. And Paul was restless and unhappy at so strange an impediment being placed in the way of his usefulness, but God revealed to him the secret—"My strength is made perfect in weakness" (2 Cor. xii. 9). Place this Divine warning side by side with old Hesiod's aphorism, and in the one we have the lesson in the form of cold heathen philosophy, in the other it is the warm, loving fulness of Christian truth. For the heathen sees man only as he is in and by himself; Christianity shows him to us in his relation to God.

The words of the narrative are in agreement with modern discoveries. Mr. Layard, in describing the remains of palaces at Nineveh, speaks of several of them as having the wall covered with lime or plaster. And here in the full light, "over against the candlestick," in a spot illuminated by the glare from one of the massive candelabra, at the top of each of which was a bowl filled with oil, and in it a bundle of flax for wick, blazing with large light, the fingers were seen, and in the expressive language of the original, "they are writing."

The king sees the fingers in motion, sees the letters being traced one by one. As he started in terror, the eyes of the revellers turned to the spot on which his gaze was fixed, and the loud mirth and noisy revelry was silenced as in a moment. There was but one thought now, as with the king they watched "the part of the hand that was writing." It was not a whole hand, but simply "fingers of a man's hand," holding probably the iron pen or chisel with which letters were traced; and all were filled with awe at the thought of what the writing might mean.

"Then the king's countenance was changed, and his thoughts troubled him, so that the joints of his loins were loosed, and his knees smote one against another" (ver. 6).

There is a swift transition from insolence to terror whenever the conscience is ill at ease. When Horace describes a man as standing fearless in the midst of the ruins of a dissolving world, he rightly says of him that he must be just. Vice can be vain and presumptuous, and in the hour of success will mock and utter words of scorn. Virtue alone can be calm and full of strength at all times, and bear prosperity without arrogance, and adversity without feebleness. Especially is virtue strong if it have for its foundation the Rock of Ages, and feel that God compasseth it about. The poor king here is as mean in his cowardice as he was arrogant in his insolence. His face a few minutes ago was flushed with wine and with pride. His colour now has fled. Pale and blanched, he can scarcely sit upright, for the joints of his body are relaxed, his knees smite together, and it seems as if he must sink down like one palsied or stricken with sudden torpor. Is this poor creature the mighty king who but a short while ago was defying the God of heaven? who was insulting Jehovah and His people? Nay, is not every one who insults God as pitiable a sight? This stroke of terror has made Belshazzar's folly plain to human eyes; but man defying God is ever the picture of impotence vainly endeavouring to match itself with the calm majesty of omnipotence.

"The king cried aloud to bring in the astrologers, the Chaldeans, and the soothsayers. And the king spake and said to the wise men of Babylon, Whosoever shall read this writing, and show me the interpretation thereof, shall be clothed with scarlet, and have a chain of gold about his neck, and shall be the third ruler in the kingdom. Then came in all the king's wise men; but they could not read the writing, nor make known to the king the interpretation thereof (vers. 7, 8).

Those who have a natural explanation ready for all miracles, suppose that as the king was drinking, his eye suddenly caught sight of some ancient bricks built into the wall, on which was some cuneiform writing, made visible by the strong light of the candelabrum; and that his guilty conscience supplied the rest, and made him think that he saw fingers actually tracing the words. But these "wise men" were well skilled in reading ancient writings, and we find that a large proportion of the works in the royal libraries were translations from older, and especially from Accadian books. Nor were these tiles or cylinders used for building materials, and had there been any inscription on the walls it would have been one in honour of the builder of the palace. Such words as Daniel read are utterly unlike any now found in the many literary treasures brought from Babylonia, nor was there any Assyrian alphabet which these men could not have deciphered. But they come and scan the strange letters in vain. The writing may have been in the old Samaritan character, which the Jews used before the captivity, during which they learned the square letters now called Hebrew. While profoundly versed in all Assyrian knowledge, it is by no means probable that the Chaldeans cared to learn the alphabets of foreign nations; and such characters as those used, for instance, upon the Moabite stone might have been outside their range of knowledge. But the writing, whatever it was, conveyed no idea to the minds of the wise men of Babylon, and Belshazzar, in growing agony and unendurable suspense, offers large rewards to the man who will allay his fears.

Dresses of honour, conveying special privileges to the wearers, were long a common form of reward in the East. Mordecai was invested in a robe of this same scarlet (Esth. viii. 15), the purple of a reddish hue being the genuine dye, and more costly and brilliant than the violet purple, usually rendered in our version "blue." But besides this and the golden necklace, the fortunate interpreter of the writing was to be, not "the third ruler of the kingdom," but one of the three chief rulers of the kingdom. In Daniel ii. 49 we read of three chief rulers of the province of Babylon. Similarly there seem to have been three who were over the whole realm. But when Belshazzar made the offer his realm was sadly shrunken. It was bounded by the walls of one city, and all outside was in the power of an enemy against whom his father had striven bravely, but in vain.

But the promises avail nought. The wise men look and look in vain. The thousand lords all look, but the writing defies their efforts, and the king's despair grows more dark and gloomy. "Then was king Belshazzar greatly troubled, and his countenance was changed in him, and his lords were astonied" (ver. 9).

How changed the scene! There had been, at first, impiety and sacrilege. They drank in the holy vessels to the honour of their gods, and indulged in light jest at Jehovah and bitter contempt of His people. And then as the carouse went on, there rose the sound of coarser revelry, and the tongue, loosed by the wine from its ordinary restraint, gave utterance to words of shameless blasphemy and ribald license; and then came silence. Every eye was turned towards the bright space illuminated by the candlestick. What can those fingers be tracing? What can those characters mean? What is the message that has come? They look towards the royal throne, but there is no comfort there. The king, lately so defiant, sits shrunken and doubled up, with terror making every limb to shake. The wise men come in. They gaze: they confer among themselves. There are four words, but in what language are they written? What is the writing? What the explanation? The king urges them on. Whoever can answer shall have honours of every sort, and the highest rank and power that a subject can attain to. They were clever enough to have invented a meaning: to have said that it meant victory, and Cyrus's downfall. But a secret power withheld them. They forego the coveted honours, and own that their boasted wisdom availed them nothing. So is it ever with mere human wisdom. The crisis comes, and it is weighed in the balance and found wanting.

And so ends the banquet. The thousand lords stand about in groups, their mirth over, with no appetite for merry jest. A giant terror has entered the hall of revelry, and every heart is weighed down with a burden of fear. In the next chapter we shall see the prophet inspired of God reading the mysterious writing, and explaining to the king that the handwriting on the wall meant his own condemnation, the overthrow of his realm, and a scoffer's death.

XVI.

AN UNWELCOME EXPLANATION.

(DANIEL V. 10–23.)

JEREMIAH, the prophet of the captivity, had foretold that Babylon should fall when its princes and nobles were drunken with wine; and that their noisy revel should end in the silence of death (Jer. li. 57). And such is the scene before us. Instead of the babble of a thousand tongues there is silence. For no one can read the mysterious writing which has so strangely changed their merriment into terror. But as they stand about in groups, uncertain what to do, "the queen, by reason of the words of the king and his lords, came into the banquet house: and the queen spake and said, O king, live for ever: let not thy thoughts trouble thee, nor let thy countenance be changed."

The queen in this place was certainly the queen-mother, who in Oriental courts always holds a position of high rank. Where polygamy is the rule, a wife counts for little, but the mother of the reigning sovereign is sure of exercising great influence. We even find the office going on into the next reign; for Asa removes his grandmother Maachah, the wife of Abijam and granddaughter of Absalom (1 Kings xv. 2, 10), from being queen-mother, because she was given to idolatry (2 Chron. xv. 16). It thus appears that beside her natural influence she held an official rank for life. So too in Turkey the mother of the reigning sovereign is known as the Sultana Validah; and, apparently, throughout the East she occupied a definite position, with many legal privileges as well as those accorded her by the affection of her son. But if this queen-mother was Nitocris, she was personally a woman of great ability and power. As the daughter of Nebuchadnezzar she was the link between the reigning dynasty and the great founder of the Babylonian empire. Apparently, too, she had inherited some of the statesmanlike qualities of her father, while her husband Nabonidus was little more than a soldier. She may thus have been the counsellor of her son, whose early elevation to rule was evidently the result of his representing through her the great king. Naturally, therefore, Belshazzar would look to her for aid, and he looks not in vain. She may even have come because the confused noise and exclamations of many voices

AN UNWELCOME EXPLANATION.　　229

had reached her apartment. At all events, "by reason of the words of the king and his lords" means "because of their loud talking," though very probably some messenger brought her an account of what had happened, and told her of her son's distress, and that the wise men could do nothing to allay his terrors.

She comes, therefore, and says, "There is a man in thy kingdom, in whom is the spirit of the holy gods; and in the days of thy father light and understanding and wisdom, like the wisdom of the gods, was found in him; whom the king Nebuchadezzar thy father, the king, I say, thy father, made master of the magicians, astrologers, Chaldeans, and soothsayers; forasmuch as an excellent spirit, and knowledge, and understanding, interpreting of dreams, and showing of hard sentences, and dissolving of doubts, were found in the same Daniel, whom the king named Belteshazzar: now let Daniel be called, and he will show the interpretation."

Now here one or two difficulties have been made. For, first, it has been asked, Why, if Daniel was master of the magicians, had he not come in with them? But probably this title was rather a high rank conferred upon a political personage than a practical matter of ordinary duty. Daniel had studied in the college of the Magi, had learned their wisdom, and by interpreting Nebuchadnezzar's dream, had proved that he excelled his teachers ;· but he was forthwith entrusted with political power, and his duties became those of a secretary of state. He retained his rank as "Master of the Magi," and in great court ceremonials might appear at their head, but he practised none of their arts. He had higher and more important functions. And when at the death of Nebuchadnezzar, or upon the murder of Evil-Merodach, all political power passed from his hands, he would neither wish himself, nor would the ordinary Chaldean soothsayers desire, that he should actually interfere with their duties. His safety in troubled times, when usurper was struggling with usurper, would be to dwell quietly ; but evidently he had the entire respect of Nitocris, and probably her protection.

But it is also asked, How was it that Belshazzar knew so little about him ? Why did he not send for him himself ? But, as we shall see, he had a general knowledge of him as one who had been in office under his grandfather ; and a young Oriental despot was not so carefully educated as to know very much even of the history of the time immediately preceding his own. There was no one round him who would care to tell him much about the statesman who had done such good service in days gone by. When Neriglissar murdered the son of Nebuchadnezzar new men would come into power, and it was as much as the old ministers could expect if they were not put to death together with their master.

But Nitocris remembered with respect one who had served her father so well, and she dwells upon his merits, not because he was a person altogether unknown to Belshazzar, but because he was a Jew; and it could not but have been a humiliation to the king to have to send to a Jew for help, when the very purpose of the festival had been to insult the Jewish God. As it is, the form of Daniel's answer is not friendly, nor could Belshazzar have expected either respect or friendship. But, as Nitocris pointed out, Daniel was the one man who had the necessary skill, and the banquet prepared in mockery of the Jews, and to pour upon them scorn and insult, is hushed, that a Jew may interpret the message sent by Israel's God.

It was probably the fear of objection being made because of his nationality that caused Nitocris to dwell so fully on his wonderful power of interpreting dreams and solving riddles and explaining things difficult and uncertain. She even commends him to her son by showing that his name was almost identical with the king's own. Both were "princes of Bel," and Daniel's Babylonian name would suggest that he was in some way one of themselves, and one who had been at least adopted by them. And so, though the king knew that he belonged to a suspected race, he yet makes no objection. Probably his anxiety to know the meaning of the strange words overcame all other misgivings.

"Then was Daniel brought in before the king. And the king spake and said unto Daniel, Art thou that Daniel, which art of the children of the captivity of Judah, whom the king my father brought out of Jewry? I have even heard of thee, that the spirit of the gods is in thee, and that light and understanding and excellent wisdom is found in thee." And then the king tells him how all the wise men of Babylon had tried to decipher the mysterious writing, and had failed, and repeats the offer of ample honours if Daniel can once again, as in old times, solve the perplexing difficulty.

The king evidently had some knowledge of Daniel. His connection with Nebuchadnezzar had been too remarkable for his name not to be from time to time upon the lips of men; but the events themselves told from mouth to mouth became probably so changed and altered, as to be but myths and fables, which the people had shaped into accordance with their own ideas. A very few years suffice for such changes, and Daniel probably lived at Babylon as one whom the people regarded with awe, as a being invested with extraordinary powers, and who had done marvellous things. But he lived there as a man laid by, who belonged to a former state of things, of which men scarcely dared to speak. Still, when the old man appeared in their streets, they would call to mind their famous king, in whose reign they were masters of the world, and would gaze respectfully upon his prime minister. And now, as again and again in old times, he had been called in to solve the mental difficulties of Nebuchadnezzar, he stands before the unworthy grandson and hears his narrative, and looks reverently upon the writing still illuminated by the blazing light of the candlestick.

He sees at once its meaning, and will interpret it, but rejects decisively the gifts. "Then Daniel answered and said before the king, Let thy gifts be to thyself, and give thy rewards to another; yet I will read the writing unto the king, and make known to him the interpretation."

The purpose of this rejection of the royal gifts was not to vindicate Jewish prophecy from the charge of being venal. No such idea was present in the mind either of the king or of the nobles.

Their one wish was to have the writing interpreted. We find afterwards that Daniel submitted to the wearing of the robe and chain of office, though he knew how worthless the gifts were. His present refusal was intended, first, to prepare the mind of Belshazzar for the boding of evil; and, secondly, as a reproof. The idea of some commentators that the king would immediately fall into a rage, and order Daniel to be punished, is without reason, nor need Daniel's words be softened down. They are too unlike those addressed to Nebuchadnezzar (chap. iv. 19), when evil was impending over him, for us not to recognise the difference. As a matter of fact, in all despotisms free language is often addressed to the sovereign, and truth is spoken in a blunt way not usual in courts where behaviour is a matter of etiquette. The history of the Arab chalifs abounds in pointed sayings that must have stung, but which it was the rule to bear. And here Daniel was one who had been the chief minister of the king's grandfather, and who, while refusing the king's gifts, was willing to do his pleasure, and set his mind at rest.

But Daniel would have been untrue to his high office if he had not reproved the king. His whole address is one of earnest rebuke and remonstrance. From first to last his words are stern, and such as might have moved the wrath of a despot; but had not that just happened which had crushed the king with terror? There is often even a relief in a small annoyance coming to divert the thoughts from a great calamity. Belshazzar had just seen the fingers writing their message upon the wall. He knew that it was a message of punishment from the God of Israel, whose holy vessels he had just been profaning. He expected only words of woe and wrathful tidings from Israel's prophet, and the rejection of his gifts was in harmony with his own secret thoughts.

And then Daniel recalls to his mind the history of the strange humiliation which had befallen Nebuchadnezzar because of his pride. "O thou king, the most high God gave Nebuchadnezzar, thy father, a kingdom, and majesty, and glory, and honour: and for the majesty that He gave him, all people, nations, and languages trembled and feared before him: whom he would he slew; and whom he would he kept alive; and whom he would he set up; and whom he would he put down. But when his heart was lifted up, and his mind hardened in pride, he was deposed from his kingly throne, and they took his glory from him: and he was driven from the sons of men; and his heart was made like the beasts, and his dwelling was with the wild asses; they fed him with grass like oxen, and his body was wet with the dew of heaven; till he knew that the most high God ruled in the kingdom of men, and that He appointeth over it whomsoever He will."

The history of Nebuchadnezzar's malady would be long remembered in the royal house, and be narrated, with such changes as are sure to accompany oral tradition, among the stories wherewith people who have no books while away their time. But no change could make it more startling than the simple facts, and Daniel magnifies Nebuchadnezzar's authority and dilates upon his grandeur to show that it was no common king who had suffered this humiliation. Belshazzar had not attained to such power as that wielded by his grandfather. He had not his splendid ability; had achieved no victories; had no army of veterans irresistible in battle, and whose sole law was the will of their lord. Very probably even there were with him one or more officers who represented Nabonidus, and as long as the father lived, there was a limit to the authority of the son. True, that they were now kept apart, and nobody within the walls of Babylon could vie with Belshazzar. But the presence of the enemy, the necessity of making resistance, the control of the army, the maintenance of its efficiency, and the prevalence of general disaffection, making all things more difficult, were so many limits of the king's power. Nebuchadnezzar had overcome all resistance, success had crowned his efforts, and difficulties had but proved his ability. Such a one could kill and keep alive; could set up and pull down. But wherever the monarch is not a person of high intellectual and moral ability, the presence of difficulties is apt to raise up some one, who, by the force of his nature, becomes predominant, and who, though still a subject, yet wields all real power.

Such may have been the case with the young king, but it was not so with Nebuchadnezzar. And yet when that grand monarch gave way to pride and arrogance, he suffered a reverse so marvellous and extraordinary, that the story of one so highly endowed, so strong in mind and will, giving way to the strangest hallucination, and roaming about lowing like the oxen and eating their food, and yet finally returning to his kingdom:—this, with the many minor events and anecdotes, which filled up the outline preserved to us in Holy Scripture, must have been repeated from father to son through many generations; and well was it if until it passed away it remained as a lesson against that sin which especially besets men in high rank and power.

There is one added particular not given in the fuller narrative, namely, that Nebuchadnezzar's "dwelling was with the wild asses." Now the wild ass is an animal difficult and almost impossible to tame, of great fleetness, wary and hard to approach, and whose home is in the desert. Living with them it would be no easy matter to approach Nebuchadnezzar; nor is it contrary to what has happened in other well authenticated cases, to believe that after a time a wild man would almost rival them in speed and certainly in endurance. At a distance, then, from the cultivated fields watered by the canals of Babylonia, far away in the deserts which border upon it, Nebuchadnezzar passed the seven years of his malady. What steps his wife and Daniel could take for his protection, and what help they could give him when consorting with these strange companions, it is difficult to say. But doubtless they would watch over him, would observe his haunts, and do all that was possible to alleviate his state.

But how constantly is it the case that men know the words of a lesson but do not understand its meaning. Too often, not children only, but grown men, learn by rote, and can repeat the sounds, but the sense is hidden from them. Even religious men may read their Bibles times without number,

AN UNWELCOME EXPLANATION. 239

and yet have seen only the casket which contains the jewel; until it may be some trial comes, some mental striving and searching of heart, and then some text, which they have repeated hundreds of times without any special meaning, is unlocked, and they find in it some deep lesson of strength and comfort, of which before they had been unaware. Widely apart are the two kinds of knowledge. Our intellects explain to us the outward form, the relations of the words, their grammatical import; it is when our hearts take them up that we learn their spiritual and Divine teaching. Belshazzar probably had often listened with curious interest to the story of his illustrious grandfather's malady, as it was repeated perhaps in the women's apartments in his childhood; and in riper years he may have read the proclamation which the penitent monarch published after being restored to his throne. But he listened as David had listened to Nathan's story of the ewe lamb; there was nothing to say to him, "Thou art the man." But the aged prophet, speaking with all the weight of one who had been the counsellor of the great founder of the Babylonian empire, now drives the barbed arrow of reproof deep into his conscience. He repeats to him the history of Nebuchadnezzar's pride and punishment, and adds,

"And thou his son, O Belshazzar, hast not humbled thine heart, though thou knewest all this; but hast lifted up thyself against the Lord of heaven; and they have brought the vessels of his house before thee, and thou, and thy lords, thy wives, and thy concubines, have drunk wine in them; and thou hast praised the gods of silver, and gold, of brass, iron, wood, and stone, which see not, nor hear, nor know: and the God in whose hand thy breath is, and whose are all thy ways, hast thou not glorified."

These are stern but faithful words, worthy of God's prophet, and the remembrance of the terrible malady with which Daniel's God had smitten the most mighty monarch of his race must have repressed every rising of the king's anger, and humbled the arrogance which, an hour or two ago, had been so rampant. It is a well-known rule that those who are insolent in prosperity are abject and mean when distress overtakes them. For the arrogance and the meanness are alike the oscillations of a mind destitute of self-control. The pendulum which goes farthest in one direction swings equally far upon the opposite side. Belshazzar was too terrified by the apparition of the fingers writing his condemnation to dare say one word of remonstrance. In his pride he had defied God, but his pride is quelled, and he meekly listens as the prophet rebukes him;

tells him of knowledge unused, and of the warning, unheeded, of Nebuchadnezzar's punishment; stigmatises as things void alike of sight and hearing and sense his idols of silver and wood and stone; and warns him that the God against whom he had lifted himself up was the God in whose hand was his very breath, and who had the control of all his ways.

Well would it be if we would each one learn the lesson of bowing in humble obedience to God's will from these examples of old, instead of having it forced upon us by personal suffering. Or rather, as Christians, it is our duty to bend to the Divine will in loving trustfulness as being the will of our Father which is in heaven. Too often men will learn nothing except by their own experience, and it is only when battered and bruised by vain striving, and humbled by disappointment and failure, that man's self-will is content to lose itself in the love of One whose mercies fail not. But here the lesson was of punishment alone. Humbled, terrified, but unrepentant, Belshazzar listens to his doom. And as Daniel spake the words of interpretation, already the storm was gathering close around that was to sweep him away. And again and again, it may be, the words of Daniel resounded in his ears: "The God in whose hand thy breath is, and whose are all thy ways, thou hast not glorified."

XVII.

MENE, MENE.

(Daniel v. 24-31.)

IN the previous verses Daniel had narrated to Belshazzar the history of Nebuchadnezzar's pride and mysterious punishment. And of this, more or less, the king had already known, and yet he had given way to a more impious arrogance than that which had caused his grandfather's humiliation. And therefore had this strange sight come to him of the part of a hand writing his condemnation upon the wall. We need not waste time in considering whose hand it was; whether it were that of an angel, or whether it were some special creation called into being for temporary use. Enough to know that by the wondering eyes of the king and his lords fingers had been seen tracing strange characters, and that the characters remained visible. The particles of matter of which the plaister was composed had grouped themselves as God willed, even though it had been a spiritual hand that moved them, and they bore their silent message to the terrified revellers. And the first word, twice repeated, was Mene. "And this is the interpretation of the thing: MENE; God hath numbered thy kingdom, and finished it."

Literally the word means: Numbered, numbered. There is an appointed measure, a settled limit to everything. Even in the creation of the world, and the constitution of matter, number plays an important part. For it is by the arrangement of a few elementary particles according to fixed numerical proportions that the endless variety of substances here on earth is produced. Chemical affinities, which regulate the composition of most of the things around us, so work by numbers that the formula in books of chemistry descriptive of most substances is even given in figures. Music, again, depends upon vibrations numerically different; and in the solar system the distance of the planets from one another is in a settled numerical ratio, so that even before so many asteroids were discovered, it was known that a planet must once have existed in the space which they now occupy; for otherwise there would have been a gap in the numerical order. When, then, we look out upon the world around us, we may say, Numbered, numbered. All is by number and weight.

And this is true, not merely of matter, but in a still higher sense of our lives. Our days are numbered, and come to an end as soon as their tale is told. We start with an allotted sum, and as soon as the total is reached, we pass away. Our acts are numbered. But here the sense is different. Of our acts a record is kept, and not one of them passes away from remembrance, while the length of our lives is settled for us at the very moment when we begin our course. But here we may imagine some one asking, Who is it that gave man this allotted space of life? Who is it that now keeps record of all his doings? And we may answer, Even He who made the world by order and proportion, and ordained that this mystery of number should pervade it everywhere. A world so subtilly constituted can be no chance product; and if made on a settled plan, then we may be sure that it had a settled purpose also; and that purpose can be nothing less than the trial and probation of the one being who walks upon it erect and self-conscious—even man.

For God's people there is comfort in the thought that all things are counted, and for this purpose our Lord used it. Man need not live careworn and anxious, for the very hairs of his head are all numbered. He is not subject to blind chance. His existence is not the result of a mere fortuitous medley, nor can he ever become the victim of luck or accident. But more than this. To the heathen life was often made very miserable by the supposition that he was the prey of destiny. He seemed made only to be crushed by forces over which he had no control, and which moved on dark and pitiless, unmoved by human joy and sorrow. To the heathen nothing was more painful than the sight of a good man suffering adversity, and their poets, therefore, took it as the general subject of their tragedies, because it so deeply agitated the mind, and filled it with terror. It causes no terror now, for to the Christian it brings the thought of "a far heavier weight of glory." For us there is neither chance nor destiny. Not chance, for all things are numbered. God, by settled rule and measure, allots to each thing its place and time, and nothing happens but as He wills. Not destiny, for human actions are counted. And they are counted because in every one of them man has something of his own. If man were subject to fate and necessity this would not be so. No more account would be taken of actions irrevocably fixed by destiny than of the ticking and striking of a clock. But man has the high privilege of being a fellow-worker with God. Made in God's image, he has something of that originating power, something, also, of that regulating power, which in the highest degree belong to God. By this power God created the world; man by it alters and shapes and moulds things around him, and forms his own character. And because man thus has in him something Divine, because, in his free energy and power of thinking and choosing and acting for himself, he is a " partaker of the Divine nature " (2 Pet. i. 4), therefore none of his acts are lost or forgotten, but they are written in the book of remembrance that is before the Lord continually.

But men may live thoughtless and forgetful of this high value of their acts. Made in the likeness of God, they may debase themselves, and abuse their noble gifts to their own shame and condemnation. And if the probation of man, and his endowment with attributes, resembling in their degree those of Deity, was intended for his good, and his final elevation to transcendent glory, then must also his misuse of them end in lasting misery. And so to Belshazzar the words brought only grief and consternation. Numbered, numbered. His days were numbered and over. His joys numbered and gone. His kingdom, his royal dignity and reign, numbered and taken away. No more life, no more pleasure, no more feasting and revelry, no more regal state and pomp of grandeur. He had reached in all things his allotted number, and what remained? What was the end of all his opportunities? The account must now be summed up, the columns balanced; and what was the result? Belshazzar could have had little hope, but the prophet kept him in no suspense: "TEKEL; thou art weighed in the balances, and found wanting."

Counted and weighed. Oh! that men would feel their responsibility while still it is the day of grace. To a heathen, perhaps, this idea of responsibility was something novel. He knew, indeed, that there was retribution, that evil deeds followed and overtook the guilty perpetrator, though by a slow and unsteady step. Yet they did recognise a connection between virtue and happiness, between vice and misery, and did understand that there was a just government actually in exercise here on earth. "Rarely," says the epicurean poet, Horace, "does punishment fail to reach the guilty, though it follow with lazy tread." Still to the heathen much was dark. He saw sorrow and trouble falling where they were not deserved. He saw men in high places who neither merited their elevation nor used their power for good purpose.

Though traces there were of a just ordering of things, yet the ordering was not exact or unfailing, and there was much of which he could give no explanation. For us all this has changed. This world is not to us our whole field of view. The Christian sees time in its relation to eternity, and his present life is but a beginning, a prelude, a preparation for the life beyond the grave. When, then, with Isaiah, he exclaims, "Thou, O most upright, dost weigh the path of the just" (chap. xxvi. 7), the thought to him is full of joy and confidence. For he feels that in this preparatory world God is with him, ordering his steps, noting all his difficulties and trials, aiding him by His grace, and admitting him for Christ's sake to a covenant of love, whereby in that future world his happiness will be made sure.

But for Belshazzar there was no comfort or joy in this even balance of God's justice. For he had been weighed and "found wanting." His life had been short; only a very few years had been allotted him, and he had reached the end; and now he must be put into the scales, and his acts weighed. He had been a king, and how had he used his power? On the one side were his opportunities—they had been many, and pressed the scale low down. On the other side, how many were his acts of mercy? how many his deeds of justice? Where were his thoughts for the welfare of his people? his resolutions to reign for their good, and to exercise vigilant self-denial, lest base pleasures and greed of power and wealth should make him their scourge instead of their protector? He had been appointed by his father to share the regal power at a time of difficulty, when a powerful enemy, who had conquered most of Asia, was active in the field; and when his subjects, harassed by unrighteous oppression, were eager to cast off the rule which his father had usurped. What had he, with a better claim to the throne, done to lighten the burdens of the men who had served his grandfather, to improve their condition, to lessen their discontent? He was but a mere youth, but already a voluptuary. Wives and concubines had been gathered for his pleasures; but we read of no wise step taken by him for the nation's good, of no brave energy used in the nation's defence. But amid the low rumblings of the earthquake, warning him that some dreadful convulsion was at hand, he makes a great banquet that he may insult a brave but fallen nation, now incorporated among his subjects, and that he may add to his voluptuousness and sloth the graver sins of impiety and sacrilege.

"Found wanting;" such was the verdict of

justice after carefully weighing his dangers and his difficulties, the excuses that might be made for him, even his natural defects of character, and all that could be said in his defence. Even of the heathen God is a lenient judge, and long-suffering; nor does He exact of any that which is beyond their powers. Of this untutored youth He would require far less than of us; for the stripes of punishment are few or many according to the knowledge that men have of the Divine will. But whatever be the measure of our knowledge, finally for all, the time of weighing comes, and we shall have to give account of the grace vouchsafed us, of the aid which God grants to His people, and of the full knowledge bestowed upon us of the way of salvation through Jesus Christ our Lord. Well may the thought of this weighing make us humble and careful, yet full of calm hope, as we call to mind God's many mercies. Here one was weighed whose path had been illuminated by no such bright light as shines upon us; and had there been in him a love for righteousness, the verdict would have been one of mercy; but "he was weighed in the balance and found wanting."

"PERES; Thy kingdom is divided, and given to the Medes and Persians." In verse 25 the writing is said to have been "Upharsin," literally "and dividers," but with an evident allusion to the Persians. Here, nevertheless, we find the Medes (or Madai, as they are called in the cuneiform inscriptions) placed first, while in the Book of Esther Persia has the supremacy (Esth. i. 3, 18, 19), as that state, after a very few years, deprived the Madai of their ascendency. Even then, in this slight matter, we cannot help noticing the extraordinary accuracy of Holy Scripture; and had the Book of Daniel been written, as the negative critics assert, in the time of the Maccabees, the writers would naturally have used the order of precedence which had then long been current.

Instead of Upharsin, Daniel takes the singular *Peres*, a passive participle signifying "Divided," and so agreeing with Numbered, Weighed. Now the reason of this change may be to show that the time of fulfilment had actually come. The king knew before that outside the walls were men eager to strip him of his realm and share it among themselves. And Daniel says that it is done. The numbering is over, the weighing finished, and because he has been found wanting, the sentence must at once be executed. His kingdom is taken from him, and divided between the Medes and Persians.

The interpretation is over; the dread meaning of the words explained; Belshazzar is a king no longer, and his realm is bestowed upon his foes. But still he keeps his royal word. Unbending and stern as had been the prophet's words, yet must he have the stipulated reward. "Then commanded Belshazzar, and they clothed Daniel with scarlet, and put a chain of gold about his neck, and made a proclamation concerning him, that he should be the third ruler in the kingdom."

For Belshazzar to have withheld the promised honours would have been unworthy of a king, and he may possibly have even hoped to propitiate Israel's God by honouring His prophet. For Daniel to have refused them would have been churlish and altogether wrong. True, he had haughtily put them aside when as yet no one knew what the strange writing might mean; but after words of such utter condemnation and the foretelling of so miserable a reverse of fortune, it would have been mean, and a sin against charity, unnecessarily to grieve and harass the king, and put himself in hostile opposition to him. And, moreover, the fact that Belshazzar had conferred upon him these high honours would be witness to the reality of what had occurred. The news of it would doubtless be carried to the conquerors, and the great favour shown by Darius to Daniel, and by Cyrus to the Jews generally, was very probably connected with

Daniel's interpretation of the handwriting. For from the date of the death of Evil-Merodach until now the prophet had been living in seclusion. Most men probably knew of him only as one of the great men of Nebuchadnezzar's time. Suddenly under the Medes he is the trusted counsellor of Darius. Now, even if the Jews had been strong partisans of the invaders, and prime agents on this eventful night, it would not be enough to explain the elevation of Daniel to so high a post under the conquerors. But if the story of this banquet were told, with all the particulars of the king's terror, and the failure of the wise men of Babylon to read the mysterious writing, and the testimony of Nitocris to Daniel's ability, and his interpretation of the words, attested by the royal gifts and honours; Darius, when he learned all this, and the meaning put upon the writing, predicting his immediate victory, would surely wish to know more about this great sage, and would inquire into his past history. And thus, when we reflect upon the narrative, we begin to see that the purpose of this occurrence was not merely the vindication of Jehovah's majesty and the punishment of sacrilege, but was part of that mysterious Providence which watched so carefully over the fortunes of the Jews at Babylon.

For the exile at Babylon was a formative time, like the sojourning in Egypt. By the latter Israel was made into a nation; at Babylon it was formed into a church. It went there weighed and found wanting; it returned stamped with deep penitence and earnest piety, and cured of its love for the base pleasures and the superstitions of idolatry. And of this change Daniel was the chief instrument. His great authority and power at the court of Nebuchadnezzar was bestowed upon him not merely that he might protect God's people, but that his own personal piety and that of his companions might the more deeply influence the minds of his countrymen. And when for many years he had been moulding them afresh to God's service, he was laid aside. His work seemed done, except so far as he could influence them by setting them the example of a pious life in a position of comparative obscurity. Israel learned, during this period, to stand alone, and to depend upon itself. And this seclusion continued for nearly twenty years, and then a new time of change and public trouble arrived, and Daniel was suddenly called out of obscurity by the Babylonian king. Belshazzar's last act was to remove the veil which had so long concealed the great Hebrew who, in the crisis of their first removal to Babylon, had been the strength and comfort of his people, in order that he may again be their stay in the transference of empire to a new race, and aid in bringing about their return to their old country, though too advanced in years to accompany them in person.

We cannot then regard Daniel in any other light than as one specially raised up to work that change in the heart and inner life of the Jewish Church which was effected at Babylon, and which was, in fact, the great purpose of the exile. And just as the former marvellous occurrences during the reign of Nebuchadnezzar were divinely ordered to invest Daniel with power and influence to be used for the good of the Jews during their seventy years' banishment from their country, so this event was for the furtherance of their return to their land. As for Belshazzar, his sins and impiety were justly punished, but the handwriting had higher purposes than to warn him and lead to his repentance. He had no such grand qualities as those which distinguished his grandfather, and his record is abruptly closed. "In that night was Belshazzar the king of the Chaldeans slain. And Darius the Median took the kingdom, being about threescore and two years old."

Even before the discoveries of the Cyrus cylinders, it was the opinion of commentators that Belshazzar's death was the result of a conspiracy, and that this great banquet, and the summoning of a thousand lords from their posts, gave the desired opportunity for the attack. Some even of the lords present may have been among the conspirators, and the confusion and excitement and dismay which followed upon Daniel's interpretation of the writing may have encouraged them to carry out their plans at once. And so, while some opened one of the city gates to admit the enemy, others seized upon the royal palace, and the king was slain. Thus dismally ended the banquet in which the sacred vessels of Jehovah were exposed to mockery, and the Jews scornfully reminded that the city which they so loved, and the Temple of their God, had lain in ruin for seventy years. The statement in the last verse that a particular person—Darius the Median—took the kingdom, and not the Medes and Persians generally, is intended to prepare the mind for the close relation in which we immediately find Daniel and this prince, and helps to justify our preceding remarks that the chief purpose of this miracle was the raising of Daniel to such power and authority under the conquerors as would enable him to protect the Jews; to exercise once again among them a predominant influence, and to be the instrument of carrying out the Divine purpose of restoring Israel to its land, as a necessary condition for the coming and ministry of Jesus Christ our Lord.

XVIII.

THE FALL AND RISE OF EMPIRES.

(DANIEL vi. 1–3.)

SHORT was the delay between the deciphering of the handwriting and the fulfilment of the ruin it threatened to the Babylonian empire. And Darius the Mede, having taken the kingdom, next proceeds to make wise arrangements for the orderly administration of its affairs.

"It pleased Darius to set over the kingdom a hundred and twenty princes, which should be over the whole kingdom" (ver. 1).

The head of gold, then, has fallen. The first of the four great earth-monarchies has had its little day, and the second has taken its place. It is now the breast of silver, with the strong arms of Elam and the Madai, which dominates the Eastern world, and holds the reins of empire for its allotted season.

There is much food for serious reflection in this brief record of the transference of power. Is it the will of God that the centre of earthly dominion shall be ever changing? Is first one race and then another to bear the responsibility of rule? And is the time in each case to come when the dominant power will seek to evade its responsibilities, and give itself up to the selfish enjoyment of the power and wealth already acquired? It is the pressure of responsibility which makes a nation great, as it makes a man, who has the right metal in him, great also. One who in youth is placed in a position of trial and difficulty, if he be a man of worth, rises to the level of his responsibilities, and is ennobled in character by having all that was best in him called out into active exercise. One great value of our Indian empire is that it trains so many brave men for noble work, by laying upon them when young such vast responsibilities. And that which calls forth the best energies of a man, forms also and exalts a nation if the burden be nobly borne. By the pressure of onerous duties and grave responsibilities a nation is urged onward to greatness; or if it prove unequal to the task of bearing them, it falls into the rear, and a stronger nation takes its place. For what are these responsibilities but opportunities and powers of working for God?

In the Bible we see a rapid succession of great

earthly powers. Omitting the empire of the Hittites, now so remarkably brought to light, there is, first, a long struggle between Egypt and the two Assyrian cities of Nineveh and Babylon. Finally, Babylon becomes all-powerful, but its supremacy lasts only for the lifetime of a single man. Immediately upon the death of Nebuchadnezzar internal corruption saps the power of his kingdom. Anarchy and murder prevail. Everywhere there is luxury among the rulers; discontent among the ruled, and a general loosening of the bands of society. Nebuchadnezzar, with all his greatness, seems to have had no idea of civil government. Everything depended upon the mental vigour of a despot. And when that despot was a weak voluptuary like Evil-Merodach, all went to pieces. This centralisation of power is ever the weakness of a despotism; and even when, as in the case of Napoleon I., the despot is an able civil governor, yet the concentration of authority in one hand so enfeebles the rest of the body politic, that when "the head of gold" is gone, the empire falls at once into decay. The higher the single pillar rises and overtops the rest, the more certain is its overthrow.

In the narrative before us we see that Darius was anxious to provide for the good government of his vast dominions, and to train men in the duties of political life. The Persian empire consequently had a longer duration of rule than the Babylonian, but fell finally through the ambition of its rulers and the effeminacy of its people. Next follows the outburst of Greece from its petty cradle, carrying a high civilisation with it and a glorious language as the choice gifts of its conquering arms; and finally there was the iron rule of Rome. Since the Christian era began we see a constant change going on. At one time Italy sways the destinies of mankind; then Germany under Karl the Great; then Spain, then Austria, then France under Louis XIV. In the beginning of this century France was all-powerful under Napoleon, but its supremacy has passed away, and Berlin is now the seat of the most mighty continental power. England, to whom God has given so vast a colonial empire, has attained to a foremost rank among nations only in recent times; and to us it is a serious question whether our power is temporary only, and whether the day is coming when our glory, like that of Babylon, and Macedonia, and Rome, will be a thing gone by.

Now the examples of the past all lead to the conclusion that the centre of power and influence is always shifting. But the history of Daniel teaches us also plainly two great truths: the first, that the Most High ruleth in the kingdom of men, and giveth it to whomsoever He will; and the second, that while earthly kingdoms wax and wane, there is one enduring kingdom which is ever growing, which overcomes all resistance, and which must last for ever. Now these great principles make it plain that an earthly empire will last so long as it does God's will. The continuance of England's empire does not depend upon the supply of coal and iron. It does not depend upon the energy even of its people, or the largeness of its trade, or the greatness of its colonies. All these are things useful and precious, but they will prolong our empire only if they are rightly used. The one thing that will maintain our dominion will be our obedience to God and our usefulness in carrying out His merciful purposes for the good and the salvation of mankind. Should England become a sceptical and unbelieving nation, it will no longer be capable of doing God's work, and will be laid aside. But if an empire be a trust given by God to be used for His purposes, then to refuse responsibilities may possibly be the refusal to work for God; and as a necessary result the responsibility, and with it the power of doing God's work, will be offered to some other nation. If our empire in India corrupts instead of Christianising the people entrusted to our care, the Indian empire will be taken from us and given to others. And when so given their responsibility begins, and the trial whether they are fit or not to be God's ministers and do His work. This shifting of power means the successive trial of nations by Him who ruleth in the kingdom of men; and by it they are called one by one into prominence, and made the arbiters of the destiny of feeble nations, both for their own moral elevation and for proof whether they are fit to do God's will. And if there is one grand Old Testament lesson plainly writ upon every page of that wonderful book, it is that nations prosper or decay according as they are true or false in their allegiance to Him who both made this world and now rules it for the spiritual good of His creatures.

And to this we must add the second great truth, that the "God of heaven has set up a kingdom which shall never be destroyed, nor shall it be left to other people, but it shall break in pieces and consume all earthly kingdoms, and it shall stand for ever" (chap. ii. 44). There is, then, permanence somewhere. Continuance is possible, but only in certain relations. As far as any earthly empire is doing God's work here below, so far it shares in the enduring nature of His kingdom. As far as the objects of any kingdom are the upholding of faith in God, and of virtue and morality among men, as long as its rulers promote chastity, temperance, justice, self-restraint, honesty, and other such virtues, so long it partakes of the nature of a Church, and will share in the Church's charter of continuance. Christ's Church exists for the highest of all purposes, the salvation of the souls of men; earthly kingdoms occupy only a lower sphere, and have for their immediate object the good of man in his temporal state. If the rulers have no other conception of this good than man's physical well-being, then but a brief continuance will be granted to their dominion; for it is of the earth, earthy. If they aim at the moral well-being, and the attainment of a higher degree of virtue by the people, then the state which they govern becomes in its degree a church, and will abide. But they cannot promote morality and be indifferent to religion; for there is no firm basis for morality except the fear of God.

The history of the Church teaches us the same lesson. Each national Church is a candlestick, whose one purpose of existence is to raise aloft the beacon light of Christ. Let it grow cold and selfish, and indifferent to the spiritual welfare of the masses round it; let it become formal, and

THE FALL AND RISE OF EMPIRES. 265

care more for decorous services and ritual than for winning souls for its Master; let it cease to preach the Gospel to the poor, or feed them with husks instead of the living bread and water of Bible truth, and its candlestick will be taken away. We need not go far abroad to find lands where glorious Churches once shone brightly, but which are now dominated by unbelief; and in all such lands, though the form of the candlestick may remain, no Gospel of light and truth is held aloft by it.

We cannot leave this subject without noticing another great fact in Holy Scripture, and it is this: the Jewish nation formed by God for the highest and noblest use never was a great earthly power. Under David it attained to some degree of local preponderance, but even then its dominions were very limited. I suppose that David's subjects were, at most, but a few millions. Yet in one respect the destinies of the world were in their hands; for their task was to tell men the truth about God's nature, and to teach them how to serve Him in holiness. Now, though placed in the very pathway of war between the great powers of Egypt and Assyria, yet God gave them a wonderful continuance of independent existence; but it was conditional upon their true service to Him. When He had taken them to Babylon for their moral and spiritual good, He even brought the kingdom of Nebuchadnezzar to an early end, in order that they might be restored to their own land. We know of no race which emerged from the ruins of Babylon to a renewed existence but the Jews. And now, of all the nations of whom we read in ancient history, the Jews alone survive. Arabs wander where once the Assyrian ruled; Albanians people Greece; the Romans had died out long before their empire fell under the attacks of the barbarians. The Jews lead a charmed life, and St. Paul teaches us in Romans xi. that this is so because God has still work for them to do, and purposes of mercy for them, for their fathers' sake.

We conclude, therefore, that this summoning first of one nation to the front, and then of another, is for the general progress and advancement of mankind. And next, that though earthly kingdoms rise or fall into decay, God's universal Church cannot fall, but will continue to grow and spread its influence among mankind, yet slowly, perhaps, because, as the pages of history too uniformly attest, earthly powers are more eager after wealth and extended dominion than for doing the will of God in the lands belonging to them. We have seen, too, that a very small kingdom may be God's chosen instrument for the very highest purposes, and that a very ennobling responsibility may rest upon a people which possesses no widespread dominion nor physical power. And, finally, we must urge this important point of difference between these old-world empires and Christian powers now, that they wrought unconsciously, but rulers now consciously. God had purposes for those heathen kingdoms, and Greece especially and Rome were necessary factors in the preparation for Christ's coming. But they did not know it themselves, nor could their wisest men advance farther than to general commonplaces as to the superiority of virtue over vice, and the certainty that iniquity and inner corruption prepare the way for the downfall of a state. To us so much has been revealed that the Christian statesman works consciously, and any one who is not content to regard himself as God's instrument, and be ready to do the Divine will, incurs, as the certain verdict on himself and his policy, TEKEL—Weighed in the balance, and found wanting.

This had been the verdict upon the Babylonian monarchy, and as soon as the sentence was passed the whole Assyrian race fell into decay. For centuries the mighty cities on the Euphrates and Tigris had dominated the Eastern world. They stood on the highway of the trade between the East and West, and the manufactures of Greece crowded their marts side by side with the produce of the looms of India. The soil, watered by a vast network of canals, was fruitful beyond measure, and the teeming population supplied their chiefs with armies wherewith to enforce their rule on nations far and wide. The cuneiform inscriptions show how cruelly they had desolated the regions around them, and how, for century after century, they had been a scourge to mankind. Now all is over. Never since the day of Belshazzar's feast has the seat of empire been situated in the Mesopotamian plains. It is transferred, for the present, to the races inhabiting the hills of Elam and Media.

And while the real power rested with Cyrus, a shadowy Darius held the reins of nominal authority, with, possibly, some measure of administrative command. Mr. Sayce asserts that according to the cuneiform inscriptions the Persian empire was really founded by Darius, the son of Hystaspes. The king here mentioned is not the Persian son of Hystaspes, but a Mede, and apparently Cyrus used him for the internal management of the kingdom while he was occupied with war.

And with him we find ourselves on a higher level. He is not only a humane man, though one too easily imposed upon, but he is a statesman. We find that subsequently Darius Hystaspes arranged his vast dominions into twenty satrapies, with a system of posts and couriers to keep those at headquarters fully informed of all that went on. We find little statesmanship in the annals of Ninevite and Babylonian kings, and Nebuchadnezzar's system of tearing people from their homes to people his vast city was a sure way to make his conquests valueless. It deprived them of their inhabitants to surround him with bitter enemies, and fill his city with races which could never coalesce.

The more usual mode of ancient conquerors was to leave each race in possession of its own laws and customs, and to interfere as little as possible with their native rulers. But over these the hundred and twenty princes appointed by Darius would each have the supreme authority in his own district, would collect the revenues, command the army, administer justice, especially in cases of appeal, and would be careful to overawe the larger cities, and prevent them or any of the native nobility from raising the standard of revolt. But Darius attempted more than this. For he wished to bind the whole realm together, and provide means for making his princes each do his duty, and probably upon an uniform plan. "For over them he set three presidents, of whom Daniel was first, that the princes might give accounts unto them, and the king should have no damage" (ver. 2).

Now these presidents would insure a due subordination and obedience to the central authority on the part of these princes. Without it each one, unchecked and supreme in his own district, would govern after his own fancy. But the king now took care that their decrees and edicts in all matters of importance should be submitted to the presidents; and further, general orders would be sent down to them from the centre, and thus a certain degree of uniformity be secured. And of these Daniel was one, but not, as the Authorised Version says, "the first." More probably each president had his own department. They were the three principal secretaries of state, of equal rank with one another, and each bound to report to the king all matters of importance in his own special province. One would certainly have charge of the revenues, another of the administration of justice, and so on. The army was probably under the immediate control of Cyrus.

The appointment of Daniel was probably the natural consequence of the high position he had held under Nebuchadnezzar, coupled with the services of the Jews in obtaining the admission of the

Median army into Babylon, and with Daniel's own conduct upon that eventful night. And at first it was probably popular with all parties. His high fame and reputation, his noble history, his acquaintance with Babylonian policy and its rule in the days of its grandeur, and his personal dignity and great wisdom, all marked him out for eminent office. But envy gradually stole into men's minds because of his probity and success. For "this Daniel was preferred above the presidents and princes, because an excellent spirit was in him; and the king thought to set him over the whole realm" (ver. 3).

The words do not mean, as our version suggests, that Daniel was preferred by being made the first of the three presidents, but that he was so wise and thoughtful and upright, and so able and skilful in all the affairs of his department, that he grew daily in favour. The preference was gradual. Each day the king gave more heed to his advice, and in difficult matters it was to Daniel that he chiefly went for counsel. After all, this was but natural. Daniel was of great age, at least eighty. He was a man of vast experience, who had held weighty offices of trust from his youth. His younger colleagues might, at all events, have waited till the increasing burden of years made him withdraw from office. But no! They could not bear to see his growing influence with their sovereign. They belonged, most of them, to the dominant race. Like the king they were Medes. What was the good of victory if a man of a race vanquished by those whom they had conquered was to rule them? Envy is the mean reptile that ever crawls after the good and wise, when success and reputation are won by them, and tries to tarnish the lustre of their fame. So now it was creeping after Daniel; and in our next study we shall see it choosing its occasion, and gratified with a short triumph, only to fall into merited disgrace and punishment.

XIX.

THE HOUR OF DANGER.

(Daniel vi. 4–10)

IT is the penalty of greatness that envy ever follows in its path. Nor is goodness any protection. For it is not personal wrong, but the contrast between the merit that has raised to honour, and the commonplace qualities of the envier; between the success that has followed upon high desert, and the obscurity of the envier's lot, that arouses his jealousy; and it burns with rage though there be no injury received, nor anything blamable in the person envied. In Daniel there was very much to abate envy. His was no sudden advancement, whereby he had been promoted over men long in the royal service; on the contrary, he had been the prime minister of the greatest of Babylon's kings. He was no young man, likely long to stand in the way of others, but one so old that naturally he must soon give place to them. Nor was his appointment contrary to policy: for he was likely to win for the new kingdom the goodwill of the many transplanted races, whose festering discontent had been the chief cause of the easy victory of Cyrus. Their envy had no just ground, but was roused and made malignant by the double fact that Daniel was a man of extraordinary merit, and that his merit was known and valued.

It was probably upon its becoming manifest that the king intended to raise him to still higher honour, and "set him over the whole nation," that the anger of the satraps became too violent for restraint. They resented it, not because they were corrupt, and Daniel's honesty kept them from enriching themselves; but more probably because they were ambitious, and deemed that it was a slight to the conquerors to give the highest office in the realm to one of a race vanquished by those whom they had now defeated. Daniel was a slave of slaves in their eyes, and was he now to rule over those who had beaten his masters? National antipathies are ever things difficult to control, with which reason has nothing to do, but which, rooted in passion, strongly bias and sway the will. And they have a good side; for patriotism is closely allied with them, and poor and barren is the nature of the man who will not bear all and risk all for his country's good. But pride of country, rather than love of it, took with these men the form of hatred and injustice, and they sought occasion against Daniel at the very time when he was doing their nation good service.

They sought their opportunity, first of all, in matters respecting the kingdom. Eagerly they watched his administration, and hoped to find something neglected, or some failure. For want of good fortune is often more severely visited upon a ruler than wilful wrong. His high rank ought to be justified by abilities which command success. There was no probability of their discovering corruption or partiality, but they did hope to find something that might have been managed more skilfully. And they sought in vain. Even with the aid of the result, which enables men afterwards to see so clearly what ought to have been done, they could detect no error, no mistake, in his measures, nor was there any fault, anything that they could fairly blame in his conduct. Eager and clear-eyed in their scrutiny they found only wisdom, justice, integrity, success; and instead of praising him and abandoning their wicked purpose, they were only the more embittered against him.

"Then said these men, We shall not find any occasion against this Daniel, except we find it against him concerning the law of his God" (verse 5).

The word used for *the law* is not the old Hebrew name Thorah, but a late word used only here and in Ezra and Esther. Of the Thorah of Moses these men knew nothing, but they had heard of Daniel's religious practices, and felt that dislike with which men commonly regard the rites and usages of other forms of worship. And one thing is very remarkable. They were convinced that Daniel so valued his prayers and devotions that he would endure any loss or punishment rather than discontinue them even for a time. Doubtless they called him a fanatic, and despised him for being narrow-minded. But fanatic is a term often applied to men of strong convictions; and Daniel, to us, is an example of the real believer, whose prayers are no hollow forms, but a true communion with God, and therefore a privilege so precious that no earthly good or pleasure is comparable with it.

In carrying out their purpose "these presidents and satraps assembled together" (or came tumultuously) "to the king, and said thus unto him, King Darius, live for ever. All the presidents of the kingdom, the governors and the princes, the counsellors and the captains, have consulted together to establish a royal statute, and to make a firm decree, that whosoever shall ask a petition of any god or man for thirty days, save of thee, O King, shall be cast into the den of lions. Now, O King, establish the decree, and sign the writing, that it be not changed, according to the law of the Medes and Persians, which altereth not" (verses 6, 7, 8).

The margin is right in rendering the Hebrew verb "*came tumultuously.*" It literally means "to storm;" and similarly the German verb *stürmen*, means "to throng," "come with a rush." Now this suggests to us the method of their action. They pretended that a sudden ebullition of feeling had arisen among them, filling them with an eager desire to honour the king with thirty days of exclusive supremacy, during which he alone should be the granter of petitions, and neither god nor man besides. The thing was monstrous and absurd. But they represented it as a sort of inspiration, by which they were lifted out of themselves and raised above the level of ordinary reasoning. Strange and even unwarrantable might seem their request, but they were urged and driven by a fervid zeal to honour their beloved Darius in this extraordinary way, and had come with a rush to the royal palace, breaking through all the usual etiquette which fenced the king's person from intrusion, in order that their desire might be carried by acclamation. There must be no weighing of arguments, but an instant concession of their unanimous wish. They had consulted among themselves, and had been moved to make this urgent demand by an outburst of feeling which had hurried their whole body to this tumultuous proceeding.

And among them were the presidents, Daniel's two colleagues in the highest office. It is remarkable that the Septuagint ascribes the whole conspiracy to these "two young men," jealous of the growing respect shown by Darius to the man associated with them. It limits also the punishment to them; it is the two presidents only, and their wives and children, who are thrown into the den of lions. But the other versions agree with the Chaldee in describing the conspiracy as general, and not only the great officers of state in civil matters, who saw in Daniel a rival, but even the satraps and pashas took part in it. For they regarded him as a man of a subject race, set over them because of his integrity and ability, matters with them of very small account compared with their pride of birth. We are not, of course, to understand that the claim of the conspirators that "all the presidents, the governors, the princes,'

&c., was actually true. We know that Daniel, himself a president, was not consulted, but probably enough of each class were privy to their deed to justify their claim to their own minds. Of course, also, the conspiracy was confined to those present at Babylon. Readily enough, perhaps, most joined in this attempt to get rid of this noble alien, and having formed their plan, they stormed the royal palace, and so wrought on the vanity of Darius that their request was granted.

For the outward semblance of the request was permission throughout a lunar month to acknowledge Darius as the sole deity to be invoked in prayer. The Persian kings claimed to be representatives of Ormazd, and as such had a sort of right to divine honours. But when kings were despotic the natural tendency of court flattery was to raise them above the level of humanity; and besides, the ancients did not draw that sharp distinction between the human and the Divine which is natural with us. Their gods were poor creatures, and it was not, after all, so very great a compliment to place a king on a level with them. The Romans had the grace generally not to do it until the emperor was dead, when it was esteemed only due civility to call him Divus. This epithet was even applied in the Church to great saints, and we read of Divus Augustinus, Divus Gregorius, and so on. But as men attained to nobler conceptions of the Deity, conscience forbade this confusing of the finite with the Infinite. In those days it was only the Jew who felt the incommensurable greatness of God; for his Jehovah was the Creator of the heaven and the earth.

To Darius this deification of his person seemed not unreasonable. His great officers were loudly clamouring for it, and it had a political value. His subjects would submit the more readily to his yoke if thus divinity hedged him around. But vanity was probably the more powerful factor in obtaining his consent. As his flatterers urged upon him this exaltation, too readily he "assumed the god," and knew not that he was really the victim of a mean trick. For thirty days he was to receive divine honours, that they might get rid of a rival; and that rival the wisest and most just and upright of the king's counsellors.

Darius must have gnawed his very fingers in vexation when he found out how he had been duped. He, a god, to fall into such a shallow pit; to be made the sole object of prayer for thirty days simply that they, his flatterers, might carry out a scheme of villainy. No wonder that his night was sleepless after he had found out their wickedness;

no wonder that he put them all to death. For they had done that which no potentate can brook —they had made him ridiculous.

But vanity is for the time in the ascendant; he listens to their tumultuous cries, fancies that he is a very god upon earth, and signs the decree, binding himself with bonds which he could not break. For, once stamped with the royal seal and entered on the records, the decree could never be recalled, but remained in force for all time.

There was some wisdom in this rule; for it saved the people from the danger of perpetual change and fickleness on the king's part. It implied also care and reflection before the enacting of a decree which the king could not withdraw. But Darius had used no deliberation. He had not even sent for Daniel, the most trustworthy of his ministers. He was satisfied with first impressions. His counsellors besought him for thirty days to be their sole god. It pleased him personally. These men must see some grand qualities in him, when they so desire him to proclaim himself divine. And the people would thus feel his greatness. Men must pray, and for a month they would address their supplications to Darius, their god, the representative, the personification of Ormazd, and for other nations, of whatever was the being they worshipped.

And the rest were well content; "Let Darius, our king-god, live for ever." One man there was, who was not content. Perhaps the Jews in large numbers followed Daniel's example; but certainly he stood firm as a believer in one God only. For "when Daniel knew that the writing was signed, he went into his house; and his windows being open in his chamber toward Jerusalem, he kneeled upon his knees three times a day, and prayed, and gave thanks before his God, as he did aforetime" (ver. 10).

Now, first of all, we see that Daniel does not go out of his way to show his determination to honour his God before his king. There is no bravado, no wilful opposition, no setting up of his own will. He simply persists quietly in a practice which he felt to be his duty, and which he could not conscientiously abandon. The worship of God was his constant habit, and he continued it, not merely because communion with God was to him happiness, but because he felt it to be a thing commanded. Come what would, he must honour God at any risk and at every cost. But he prayed where he might well have escaped observation, though still at his usual place of prayer, neither shunning nor seeking notice from others. On the flat roof of his house he had constructed a little oratory, with movable lattices to its windows. It was his closet, into which he withdrew at stated times, that he might there be alone with God. His enemies knew what was his habit, and doubtless had spies on the watch to see whether he would do as he had been wont to do before. And it came to pass as they expected. With the lattices open towards Jerusalem, he prayed to his God thrice in each day. We learn from the Psalms (v. 7; xxviii. 2, &c.) that it was an old custom of the Jews to look in prayer towards the temple, or, as more exactly expressed in Psalm xxviii. 2, "Towards the innermost place of God's sanctuary." It was God's special presence there which dictated this custom. He sat enthroned on the mercy-seat between the cherubim, and as he had deigned to take up His abode there for them, it was only due to Him to turn to the place which He had ennobled by placing there the Shechinah as the visible manifestation of His glory. When the temple was burnt by Nebuchadnezzar, that glory had departed. The loss of the Shechinah was one of the five things in which the scribes noted the inferiority of the second temple. They refused to acknowledge that to that second temple the Immanuel had come in person, and that, therefore, the glory of the second house far exceeded that of Solomon's building. For Daniel there was still the invisible and spiritual presence of God, though the type had disappeared.

We will now notice but one more thing. Daniel prayed thrice in the day. We might naturally have expected that his hours of prayer would have been those only of the morning and evening sacrifices. And consequently the objection has been made that this was not a Jewish but a Parsee custom. It appears, however, that the Persians worshipped the three portions of the day as a sort of minor divinities, and not that they worshipped at them. More probably the words illustrate a principle often at work, namely, the literal enforcement of the words of holy Scripture. David in Psalm lv. 17, says, "Evening and morning and at noonday will I pray (or rather moan), and God shall hear my voice." The Psalmist meant that continually and all the day through, the low sound of his repeated ejaculations would mount up to God. But the words suggested midday prayer as well as at the two solemn times when the lamb was offered, and we find Peter practising it (Acts x. 9) as well as Daniel. This power of God's word is marvellous, and as Daniel was probably doing what had become customary with all pious Jews, we surely gather that the words of Psalmist and Prophet had with the Church of old that same force of inspiration which they have with us. What in an ordinary book would have been a mere poetic phrase, becomes in the Bible an abiding law to God's people. It is full not merely of direct instruction, but of suggestions and hints, not obligatory on the conscience, but helpful to our soul's needs. And Daniel's prayer three times a day justifies us in similarly using for our good, and giving new applications and fresh force to words which differ from all other words by having been spoken by the Holy Spirit of God.

XX.

THE NEMESIS OF FLATTERY.

(DANIEL vi. 11–14.)

"THEN these men assembled, and found Daniel praying and making supplication before his God" (ver. 11). The word *assembled*, as we have seen on verse 6, means "to storm," or make a sudden rush upon any one. The princes, as we there read, had come in wild haste into the royal chamber, violating the strict etiquette of the Persian court, which punished even with death the unbidden entrance into the king's presence. But their haste was premeditated. If the king had time for consideration he would, they feared, consult Daniel, who was his chief officer, and even, as the Septuagint calls him in verse 13, the king's friend; and as this would spoil their plot, they came tumultuously, as men moved by an irresistible impulse, and desired for thirty days to have no god but Darius. And the weak king consented.

To be accounted divine and infallible was a bait too tempting, and so he yielded, and the retribution soon came, and the deified king found himself in a trap from which there was no escape.

And now it was Daniel whose presence they stormed. We may well suppose that they had watched him. Scholars tell us that there was a regularly organised system of espionage in the Medo-Persian kingdom. Probably it is a thing inseparable from every system of despotic government. Where freedom does not exist, and public life is suppressed, there smouldering discontent will ever seek relief in secret plotting. And the government will endeavour to counteract this by espionage. Probably in the household of Daniel, and in that of all the princes, there were spies in proportion to their rank, not because they were distrusted, but because it was part of the system to watch all in authority. And as the chief officers of the secret department were, we may be sure, privy to the conspiracy against Daniel, the reports from the spies in his household would quickly be communicated to the other nobles.

As for Daniel, he neither sought publicity nor avoided it. He was too well acquainted with the methods of Oriental government to suppose that his disobedience to the king's decree could be concealed. And if he had chosen to make excuses with his conscience, he might have argued that it would be no great harm to offer his prayers for one short month silently, and abstain from the outward forms of devotion. God sees the heart, and it is the heart He claims. But it was just because Daniel had given God his heart that he sought no evasions. He would have been untrue to his own feelings if he had cared for his own selfish ease and safety more than for God's honour. He must put God first and himself second. Still he made no parade or ostentatious exhibition of his piety, but simply persevered in his wonted habit of withdrawing to the housetop thrice in the day; and there he offered his supplications and recited his psalms of thanksgiving in the little oratory, just as he had done aforetime, with its lattices open towards Jerusalem.

Note, then, that amidst all the weighty cares and pressure of public business, this holy man found time for regular prayer. From his office, crowded with secretaries recording on tablets of clay the events notified from every part of the realm, and inscribing with their chisels on other tablets the answers given by the chief president, Daniel, to despatches from the provinces, or the king's commands to his lieutenants far and near; and from this anxious business Daniel at stated times withdrew, and his secretaries all knew the reason, and probably in his absence talked among themselves, and discussed his conduct, blaming, perhaps, his hardihood, yet respecting him, and anxious for his safety. But his thoughts were far away. As he knelt he would bend his face to the earth when asking forgiveness of sin and infirmity; and then his gaze would turn to the city so dear to every Jew because of the Temple of the Lord their God. And if Daniel sorrowed at the thought of the Temple in ruins, and of the deep silence which now for nearly seventy years had enwrapped the holy mount, where erewhile there had been all day long the sweet chanting of David's Psalms, yet there would be comfort in the thought that God's past mercies are ever the pledge of mercies in store.

We may feel sure that when Daniel thus looked towards Jerusalem he had in his heart the words of Solomon, when at the dedication of the Temple he had prayed that should Israel sin against Jehovah, and be, therefore, carried captive into a land far or near, and should there bethink them of their country, and repent, and return unto God with all their heart, and pray toward their land

and toward their city and toward the House of their God, that their God would hear them from heaven, His dwelling-place, and forgive His people their sin (2 Chron. vi. 36–39). Daniel, too, would remember Jeremiah's prophecy of the seventy years, and feel that the set time had now nearly come; perhaps, as a high officer of state, he had some inkling of the royal purpose to set Israel free, and knew that his people had well earned their restoration by the services they had rendered to the conquerors. It was hard not to be allowed to live long enough to see his countrymen raised once again from the condition of slaves to that of a free people, and to aid in this second exodus from the house of bondage. But he would have felt himself unfit for this privilege if he had purchased it by failing in his duty. He went, therefore, as usual, to his house of prayer upon the housetop, and there the conspirators, admitted by those in Daniel's household who were privy to their design, rushed upon him, and found him in the very act. Nor did he seek to conceal his conduct from them, but met them calmly in that martyr spirit, which filled with mingled admiration and rage the persecutors of the Christians.

"Then they came near, and spake before the king concerning the king's decree; Hast thou not signed a decree that every man that shall ask a petition of any god or man within thirty days, save of thee, O king, shall be cast into the den of lions? The king answered and said, The thing is true, according to the law of the Medes and Persians, which altereth not. Then answered they and said before the king, That Daniel, which is of the captivity of Judah, regardeth not thee, O king, nor the decree that thou hast signed, but maketh his petition three times a day. Then the king, when he heard these words was sore displeased with himself, and set his heart on Daniel to deliver him; and he laboured till the going down of the sun to deliver him" (vers. 12-14).

Alas, poor king! But a day or two ago he had scaled the giddiest height of human ambition. His courtiers had made him divine. They had hailed him as Darius the god! Darius the infallible! It must be very trying to an infallible personage to have any of the ills that human flesh is heir to— say a headache—and not be able to predicate for certain what will cure it. The contrast between the poor, feeble body, suffering, perhaps, from an attack of the gout, and the power of declaring *ex cathedrâ* absolute truth, must be very painful. But here there was something worse. These courtiers, who had exalted him to a level with the

Deity, now show plainly that they had done it, not for his sake, but for their own. They had snared him with his own vanity. So much adulation for bait, and when it was taken the trap would fall, and the king be caged. It was hard to find himself so very fallible, and so easily deceived. And when he called to mind the flattery that had pleased him so well, and now knew that it was not real, and inspired by his merits, but intended to make him a mere tool and cat's-paw, the remembrance must have been bitter indeed. But the rule of Medo-Persian law, which forbade the withdrawal of an edict once signed and published, rendered him impotent. He might repent, but repentance availed nothing.

We may well believe that this rule generally worked well. For, as we have seen, it was intended as an obstacle to the too hasty enactment of a law. There are always seasons of panic both with men and states, and enactments made at such times are usually fraught with evil. In a despotism, also, the monarch is ever in danger of being deceived by designing people, and cajoled for the selfish ends of others. Delay and care are thus needful and salutary. This with us is effected by requiring that an act of parliament shall be debated and passed several times before it proceed even from one branch of the legislature to another. In despotic realms the seal of the king is enough, and we learn in the Book of Esther that a decree for the destruction of a whole nation might be obtained by a court favourite, without much trouble. It was hoped, therefore, by the framers of the Medo-Persian laws, that the knowledge that a decree once signed could not be revoked, would make kings careful and anxious not to put forth hastily commands which they could not recall. But the tumultuous entry of the conspirators demanding leave to pay him extravagant honour, was too much for Darius' prudence. He fondly imagined that their flattery was genuine, and that it arose from heartfelt respect for his great qualities. And now he was "sore displeased with himself," for he felt that he had been weak indeed. He had let himself be duped. Had he reflected, his common sense would have told him that there was some covert purpose in their noisy outcry. But he had not reflected, and had let them raise him to a level with the gods, that in a few hours he might feel himself humbled to the level of a slave; for was he not now sold into their hands, to do what they wished, but what he grieved over? And all day long he fretted and mourned and sought for some means of escape from the meshes of the net in which they had entangled him. Could not his wise men devise some plan of keeping the law in the letter, and breaking it in the spirit? Might not some other decree in some indirect way make it impossible to keep the first? Portia found out an expedient to render Shylock's bond invalid. When Cambyses wanted to marry his sister, contrary to Persian law, the magi found out a law which made it possible. We find by his subsequent treatment of them that Darius did not fear these princes, but the custom of his nation he could not break. There is something grand and admirable in this, and something weak and pitiful. It is a great thing that men obey laws written and unwritten as a matter of course. It may be painful and even injurious so to do, but they obey, nevertheless. Were it not so, social life would be difficult or impossible. But men do not submit because they feel it to be upon the whole good and right that they should yield, but because habits and customs are bonds which it is very difficult to break. Many a man has destroyed himself because he had violated some rule or etiquette of his profession or of society. The shame is too great to bear, though the act in itself might have been virtuous. But men do not ask whether the rule be right or wrong. It is enough that their associates expect submission to it from them. Only a few years ago life would have been unendurable for an officer who had refused to fight a duel; but since then moralists have leavened society with a purer creed, and broken this chain of bondage. Now Darius was in much the same state as that of an officer who, fifty years ago, had been challenged to fight a duel. He did not at all like it. In this case he knew that he had been deceived, and tricked into being a party to a deliberate murder. Yet he could not withdraw, and murder seemed better than to violate the etiquette of the kingdom. In fact, he imagined that he had no choice. So Herod was grieved when his rash promise was abused by Herodias; and yet he put John Baptist to death rather than have it said that he had broken his word. In both it was a case of conscience, of conscience misinformed and unenlightened, but those were not days when an immoral act was as such unlawful and out of the question. Nor had people then much respect for the rights of others. Daniel must die a malefactor's death because the king's conscience would not permit him to violate a state rule. John Baptist must die because Herod's conscience would not let him break his promise. Both grieved at what they had to do, but both obeyed a call to do what they supposed to be right, just as a man accepted a challenge, because the act was believed by him to be a duty. But neither Darius nor Herod had advanced so far along the road of morality as to know that they had no right to shed innocent blood. Both were unwilling agents, but neither rebelled. It was a terrible crime which each committed, and each shrunk from it, but yet did it in the belief that it was something due to their kingly office.

It is a remarkable saying of the philosopher Kant, who had advanced no further than a belief in a moral law of nature, that Christianity alone had enabled the light within us correctly to distinguish between right and wrong. Kant did not believe in the divinity of Christ, nor in the inspiration of the Apostles; but he saw and acknowledged that the morality of the New Testament was something infinitely more pure and unselfish and ennobling than that attained to by any heathen moralist. And the law of our moral nature, thus cleared and raised and enlightened by Christ's teaching, seemed to him now enough. Man, he said, needs no more. He did not see that man needs also a motive, and a power to make him love and obey the moral law. Men do not sin because they imagine sin to be virtue, but because the temptation and the desire overpower their better feelings, and each time they fall they sink to a lower level, and become an easier prey to meaner temptations. The strength of Christianity lies not in its pure morality, but in Christ's death; and its lessons of holy living are for those who have died with Christ to rise again by the power of His resurrection to a spiritual life.

To Darius no such lessons of pure morality had been revealed, nor had he been taught the secret of a renewed life. His conscience was unenlightened, yet there it was. He had been brought up to regard a royal decree as a thing inviolable. To recall an edict was a crime such as no king before him had committed. He could not do it. It seemed to him a smaller crime to shed innocent blood than to break through this hereditary custom. And so all day long he racked his brain for some expedient, for some way of solving the dilemma; but none could be found. His friend, his wise counsellor, must be sacrificed, and all because he had swallowed the bait of a coarse flattery. A day or two ago he had fancied himself a god; and now he felt himself a dupe, and "fallen from his high estate."

So generally our sins and even our follies punish us with just retribution. For vain Darius there was self-contempt; for Herod, pleased with wanton dancing, there was the sight of the gory head of one whose counsels he had often heard gladly. The graceful witchery of Salome's movements pleased for the moment, but memory would not care to treasure them up; while conscience would often bring before the gaze of his mind the ashy features of the man whom he had respected, and who had seemed to him to occupy so far higher a moral elevation than his own. By a just retribution God uses our own vices and weakness as the scourge wherewith He punishes us. Were we wise we should take the warning. But it is in vain that the moralist warns us that only the edge of folly's cup is tinged with honey, and that the long draught which follows ever grows in bitterness, and must be drained to the last foul dregs. But this, with us, is not inevitable. We do not stand, like Darius, sorrowful, reluctant, displeased with ourselves, labouring to escape, but with no outlet for deliverance. For us Christ has died, and He is our way of safety, our door for admittance into the fold of the free, and also our strength. For He does not command only, but enables us to obey. He gives swiftness to the weary feet, power to the feeble arms, peace to the aching heart. And to those who accept Him He gives the glad power to exclaim, "I can do all things through Christ that strengtheneth me."

XXI.

THE RIGHTEOUS DELIVERED.

(DANIEL vi. 15-22).

THERE is much perhaps unconscious irony in the words "Then these men assembled unto the king, and said unto the king, Know, O king, that the law of the Medes and Persians is, That no decree nor statute which the king establisheth may be changed" (v. 15). Thrice in the first few words Darius is called the king. He is at the very summit of earthly power, and invested with absolute authority. All that he says is law; "whom he wills he slays, and whom he wills he keeps alive; whom he wills he sets up, and whom he wills he puts down." So vast is his authority that what he has once spoken may not be altered. It is like the voice of the Most High, and abides unchangeable for ever.

There is this difference. The word of God does not change, because God changeth not. He is perfect in all His attributes, and therefore there can be no growth of knowledge, and no variableness of sentiment, and no newness of object to alter His will. He necessarily is "the same yesterday, to-day, and for ever." Not so Darius. In the midst of his great earthly power and dominion he was but a man, full of human weakness, and swayed by human foibles. What he wishes to-day may be cast away with hatred to-morrow, or some other fancy may have taken its place. And now this attempt to make frail man's word unchangeable as the word of Deity recoils upon himself. His vanity has been played upon by astute and designing men; and he finds that this claim to the attribute of unchangeableness binds him round in fetters strong as iron, and instead of being as God he is a slave. What he idly uttered yesterday is a yoke upon his neck henceforth. For he may not break a rule handed down to him from the kings that were before him. Painful as was his situation, he could no more set himself free from bondage to his own spoken word than a courtier could violate the etiquette of the royal presence-chamber, or a lady the laws of fashion. King though he be, he must submit. The situation is not impossible now, nay, perhaps is common. For a man may easily find himself in similar straits for fear of acknowledging that he has learned better and changed his mind.

Perhaps on some public occasion he has expressed himself in strong terms, and hastily adopted some extreme opinion. He knew but one side of the question—had only heard the advocate of one party. With increased knowledge and time for calmer judgment, he becomes aware that what he affirmed was far from the truth, and he would gladly recall his assertions. Or he may have written a book, and others better informed may have criticised it and shown its unwisdom. But pride will permit no backward step. He must not lose his character for consistency. It would often be far nobler to own one's mistake, and withdraw one's hasty words; and the humiliation would purify and strengthen that part of our moral nature which before was weak. But no! Self-love is too strong. What we have said we have said. We show ourselves as unbending as the laws of the Medes and Persians, and while we preserve our consistency we condemn our truthfulness and honesty to be cast into the den of lions. Really, whenever we have made a mistake, the one right thing to do is to acknowledge it, and humbly retrace our steps.

And now the king could not retrace his steps, but must pay the dire penalty of his folly. "Then the king commanded, and they brought Daniel, and cast him into the den of lions. Now the king spake and said unto Daniel, Thy God whom thou servest continually, He will deliver thee. And a stone was brought, and laid upon the mouth of the den; and the king sealed it with his own signet, and with the signet of his lords; that the purpose might not be changed concerning Daniel" (vers. 16–17).

It was usual in old time that the order for an execution should be carried out immediately. As the king laboured unto the going down of the sun to deliver Daniel (ver. 14), it seems as if evening was the usual hour with the Medes for putting political offenders to death; or, more probably, one condemned could not be allowed to live beyond the day of his sentence. The lords, therefore, protest against longer delay, and require that their victim be cast at once to the lions. Whether these lions were kept for the purpose of such executions, or whether they were for hunting, is uncertain. If for the latter they might nevertheless be used on great occasions to execute the royal anger, whenever it was deemed expedient to strike terror into the minds of others. For this reason, perhaps, this mode of death was chosen by the conspirators as indicating to Darius the great importance they attached to the matter. The word rendered *den* does not mean an arched vault, from which idea some commentators have drawn curious conclusions about the lions being stifled for want of air, and so on. It means a cistern, or tank, and is rightly so translated in the LXX., both here and in many other places. The idea of a vaulted den is derived from an entirely false derivation, which is the more unjustifiable, as the word used here, *guba*, is common in the sense of cistern to the Hebrew, Syriac, and Arabic languages, as well as the Chaldee, which is the language of our text. Levy, who is the chief authority in Chaldee words, distinguishes the roots clearly enough, and says in his Lexicon that *guba* means "something deep." The lions were kept in what had once been a reservoir for water, and such cisterns were often of large size, as the rain falls in Palestine only in two seasons of the year, and has to be stored not only for domestic purposes, but also for irrigation. In such a cistern, though the word used there signifies one of the ordinary and smaller size, Jeremiah was imprisoned (Jer. xxxviii. 6), and into another such cistern Ishmael cast the bodies of seventy murdered men (ibid. xli. 7). The Syriac Version calls both these cisterns *guba*. The cisterns in Babylonia were on an equally large scale, and were used for storing water from the time of the periodical floodings of the Tigris and Euphrates until the season came round again.

There were three hours of prayer, and if Daniel was discovered praying at noon, the conspirators must have been in eager haste when in spite of the king's reluctance they were thus hurrying their victim to death at sunset. And Daniel we may feel sure was calm and tranquil in the midst of their violence and cruelty. For he lived in the daily practice of prayer. Those knees bent by him so regularly in supplication before the heavenly mercy-seat meant a life of preparedness for the better world. It was as one who every day walked very near to God, that he was permitted to speak more clearly than any other of the prophets about the resurrection. It was his office to foretell that "many who sleep in the dust of the earth shall awake, some to everlasting life, and some to shame and everlasting contempt" (chap. xii. 2). The certainty of an everlasting life was not an assured conviction of God's saints generally then as it is with us now. They felt sure of God's mercy, and that there would be some sort of waking up, when they would be satisfied with His likeness. But it was only very slowly that the veil was drawn back, and God's people permitted to have a more clear gaze into the world beyond the grave. And this privilege was granted very fully to Daniel as one "greatly beloved," and he feared not the lions' den, because death to him was not annihilation, but the passage into that happier region where the saints shine "as the brightness of the firmament."

He moves on with firm heart and tranquil step to the den of lions. Though probably not a very painful kind of death, it is one that would strongly affect the imagination. The terrible roar of these fierce creatures, their vast strength, their sudden spring, the laceration of the limbs, their angry growl as they seize and devour their prey: all this and more would be present to the mind, and beat down the courage of the bravest heart when led forward unarmed and defenceless to a death so violent. But Dr. Livingstone has assured us that when he was seized by a lion, all fear and pain passed away with the shake which the lion gave him; and he thinks that this is a merciful arrangement of the God of Nature to make the death of animals when seized by the carnivora as painless as possible. But it was meant by those men at Babylon to be a cruel and painful death, and was doubtless so regarded by those who were so unhappy as to be condemned to it. And then there was no sepulture; no laying of the mortal remains in the grave amid the tears of loving friends and relatives.

But while Daniel was brave and tranquil, the king was racked with grief. Yet he had some hope. Perhaps he had heard of the three Jewish youths walking unhurt in the midst of the fiery furnace. Too many wonderful events had happened in connection with Daniel for Darius to doubt that he was high in favour with Israel's God, and that his God was one both loving and powerful. It was not without some degree of hope that he gave him words of comfort. "Thy God whom thou servest continually, he will deliver thee."

The cistern or tank apparently was of large size, and the lions, when so numerous a concourse of people came to the entrance, would crouch in whatever cover or hiding-place there was for them. Over its mouth or entrance, constructed originally for the purpose of obtaining water from it, there was laid a stone, probably one regularly used to close it, but now more carefully secured to prevent any possibility of escape. For it was sealed with the royal signet, that no one might enter without the king's permission; and with the signet of the lords, to render any attempt on his part to rescue his faithful minister impossible. The seals of both parties were thus a safeguard against unfair dealing and interference on either side, and left Daniel with no hope of mercy except from God.

"Then the king went to his palace, and passed the night fasting; neither were instruments of music brought before him: and his sleep went from him. Then the king arose very early in the morning, and went in haste to the den of lions. And when he came to the den, he cried with a lamentable voice unto Daniel: and the king spake and said to Daniel, O Daniel, servant of the living God, is thy God, whom thou servest continually, able to deliver thee from the lions?" (ver. 18-20).

The word *dakhvan*, rendered "instruments of music," is a hopeless puzzle. The versions generally understand by it "food," "cooked meats," but the Revised Version puts in the margin "dancing girls," or bayaderes, which is the rendering of Saadias. This is a very probable meaning, but we must wait till the word appears in some cuneiform inscription for its certain explanation.

But the night thus spent fasting and without his usual amusements, was a sad change from the pride of the night before. He had then been proclaimed a very god upon earth, to whom alone for thirty days prayer was to be offered. He has now learned that this was no homage to his merits, but a mean trick, and that as the price for this adulation they had obtained from him what otherwise he would never have granted. Envious men had made him their tool in order to rob him of the wisest and most honest of his counsellors. And all the night through he tossed upon a sleepless bed, smarting with double grief. For there was real sorrow for Daniel's fate, and indignation at the injustice and spite of which he was the victim; and there was shame for his own weakness, and vexation at the ignoble part he had been made to play. But there was not absolute despair. His conduct shows that his words to Daniel were genuine. He had some hope that this God of Daniel, of whose great doings he had heard so much, would protect his faithful and pious servant. Surely those prayers, offered thrice a day, and persisted in at the very peril of his life, would not be disregarded.

The suspense was insupportable, and with the first breaking of the dawn he arose, and forgetting his royal state, went hastily to the den of lions. As he approached it his hope grew less and less. No one ever yet when made to enter that cage of fierce wild beasts, had survived destruction. The lions had often held their revel over human flesh before, and would gather to their feast, and snarl and quarrel in their haste to seize the hapless wretch cast to them. The experience of the past would make it impossible for Darius to expect this

THE RIGHTEOUS DELIVERED.   309

feeble old man to escape their hunger. And his lords and satraps as they marked his departure would quickly follow. The king could not long be left alone. And carefully as they would suppress their feelings, and compose their looks to outward sympathy with the anxiety of their master, yet in their hearts there would be triumph; and his feeble hope of Divine intervention would give zest to their enjoyment, and move them to secret mockery. They had no doubt but that they had got their incorruptible president out of the way. Ere this the lions would have feasted upon him, and now they might rob and plunder the royal treasury without fear, and use their feeble sovereign for their own greed and selfishness. Little did they imagine how closely punishment was following in the track of their sin.

No sooner has he reached the den than the king cries aloud with a lamentable voice. He cannot, nor does he wish to conceal his grief. Every hour through the sleepless night he had felt more and more strongly how unworthily he had acted, and how great was his personal loss. Still he had faith enough to come to the den of lions, and would trust no one but himself. He had learned that any one who at the royal court was incorruptible had there only enemies. There was no one but himself to care about and look after his minister's fate; and though his hope of safety for him was small, yet he had some hope, and knew that that hope would be frustrated if he sent princes and high officers to learn what had happened to the man whom he knew to be faithful to him. He uses of Daniel's God a phrase which proves that he had no unworthy conception of Him, and some reason for his hope and faith; for he calls Him "the living God." As regards this, we must bear in mind that the creed of Zoroaster, which the Persians accepted, is far more spiritual than the mythology of Greece and Rome. If Ormazd was limited in his power by reason of there being a spirit of evil which struggled with him and thwarted him, yet to Ormazd himself they applied titles which prove that they regarded him as a being infinitely pure and good. To thoughtful men there must have been something very painful in that dualism which made the Medes and Persians see in this world two mighty opposing powers struggling for mastery, and man crushed and trampled under foot in the strife. But they had noble conceptions of Ormazd, and one derivation of the name is " the great giver of life." And so then here. The God of Daniel was no lifeless idol to Darius, but a being with a real existence, like the deity whom he worshipped himself. For life means action. A state of quietude and torpor is not life, but its suspension. If Daniel's God be alive, He will now prove His existence, and save His servant. And Darius does not doubt His willingness, but asks, "Is thy God able to deliver thee from the lions?" His own god had but a limited power, and was held in check by Ahriman. Was Daniel's God similarly limited? Would the evil power prove to be the stronger, and Daniel be the lion's prey, because they were things which his God might will, but could not accomplish?

The answer is not long delayed. The voice of Daniel is heard from the den, and he says: "O king, live for ever. My God hath sent his angel, and hath shut the lions' mouths, that they have not hurt me: forasmuch as before him innocency was found in me; and also before thee, O king, have I done no hurt" (ver. 21, 22).

We may well understand the joy and also the astonishment of the king. Yes. Right had prevailed, but it was not by his agency. He had betrayed his faithful servant; but the God whose ability he had doubted, yet in whose interference he had never ceased to hope, He had delivered Daniel. In the case of the three Jewish youths, Nebuchadnezzar had seen walking with them in the furnace

One whose form was "like a son of the gods" (chapter iii. 25); and there, too, the phrase is used that "God had sent His angel and delivered his servants" (verse 28). We are not indeed to suppose here that Daniel had seen any visible appearance. His words rather point to the cause which underlies all that happens upon earth. "God maketh the winds to be His angels, and flaming fire His minister" (Ps. civ. 4). What we call natural agencies are truly and really the workings of God's presence; and the laws of the universe are almighty and unchanging because they obey the commands of Him with whom is "no variableness neither shadow of turning." The omnipresence of God is the presence everywhere of infinite wisdom and power, carrying on not only all Nature's works, but even those of which man seems to be doer. There is no power but of God, and nothing can be done apart from Him. And His will is unchanging. Every word which He spake in creation is still creation's law, and by virtue of His successive commands there is light, and an earth fitted for man's abode, and vegetation perpetually springing up, and the animal world obedient to the instincts which He has impressed upon it. In God, and by God, all things live, and move, and have their being in physical and organic nature as well as in man. Were there no God there would exist only a desolate void.

But Daniel was not thinking of natural, but of spiritual agencies, employed only on special purposes, and for extraordinary ends. These natural laws and agencies are for the maintenance of this material world, and the world exists for the training of human souls. As far as men's bodies only are concerned the laws of Nature are enough. They maintain this present state of things, and supply us with all things necessary for our bodily life. Nay, they do more. They supply us with fitting materials for our mental activity. In the world around us we have whatever is requisite for all the physical sciences. The crust of the earth is the subject of innumerable arts and studies, such as agriculture, mineralogy, geology, and the like. If we look upwards we have astronomy; if around on the formation of the composite bodies which give us our atmosphere, our oceans, and even the earth itself, we have chemistry. If we look at man we call our records of his actions history; of his motives philosophy; of his social wants and government politics. In these and all other similar things we need nothing more than natural laws as they govern things around us and ourselves. And so great is the Divine goodness that Nature, as we call it, supplies not only our needs, but gives us many pleasures, and a never-ending supply of things to think about, and classify, and observe, and learn.

And with this many of our scientific men seem content. With brave energy and unwearied labour they search out the laws which govern the world around them, and the students of social philosophy study with equal industry the laws that regulate human thought and action. But there is a question far more important than any of these. Is man simply a being of this earth? Is he the result simply of high organisation slowly moving forward by unceasing evolution to a more complex and elaborate existence, but still at last merely an organisation, and not higher in kind than the germ at the other end of the long scale? The materialist answers this question in the affirmative. Man is to him a fully developed monkey and no more. Or to speak more exactly, he is a galvanic battery, which has somehow become possessed of sensation, power of motion, and will. The Christian says that there is a difference in kind, and a gulph of separation which evolution could never cross. For him man has a spiritual as well as a material existence; not a wonderfully elaborate body only, but also a soul. This is the real point at issue. If man has not merely an existence in time, but also in eternity; if he is of God, and through God, and going to God, then miracles and revelation and supernatural agency are all not merely reasonable, but an essential part of this present scheme. Miracles and revelation are both out of the question if man is the mere result of evolution, and if evolution is the mere blind working of an impersonal power, and not the present will of God carrying out calmly and irresistibly His own Divine purpose. St. Paul formulated for our use the Christian's theory of this world, and of our relation to God, when he said to the Corinthians, " To us there is but one God, the Father, of whom are all things, and we in him : and one Lord Jesus Christ, by whom are all things, and we by Him " (1 Cor. viii. 6).

Daniel, like St. Paul, regarded God as the centre of all things. Without Him there is nothing: all is mere emptiness and non-existence, the *tohu* and *bohu* of Gen. i. 2. Though as yet unspoken, he believed the substance of St. Paul's words that "of God, and through God, and to God are all things" (Rom. xi. 36). The world is God's world, created by Him for Divine ends, and man is His special workmanship, formed for high and noble use. If we believe that St. Paul's theory of the relation of the world to God is the true theory, then there is a sufficient reason for miracle and the bestowal of knowledge by the Holy Ghost.

And because Daniel believed the world to be God's world, and himself to be God's servant, holding to Him a close spiritual relationship, therefore he recognised God's presence and agency in the course of events. God was necessarily and of right the cause of all causes. And his deliverance from the lions was God's doing. "He hath sent his angel and shut the mouths of the lions."

I will only add now that the strength of most of the arguments of materialists, and the real cause of the doubts they occasion, consists in our own want of spirituality. If our lives were lived in the power of the Spirit, and our daily walk was like Enoch's in the company of the Divine Father, agnostic and scientific difficulties would have no power over us; for they would belong to a low stage of thought and action, which we had long left behind. The spiritual life is the antidote for materialism; and our duty and privilege is to aim far higher than we too often do. For our Master has commanded us even here on earth to seek to be one with God. "That they all may be one: as thou, Father, art in me, and I in thee, that they may be one in us." It is the realisation of this union in God, and the consequent knowledge, really and personally, of the Father and the Son, which is the pledge and surety of our acceptance. "For this is life eternal, to know Thee the only true God, and Jesus Christ, whom Thou hast sent" (John xvii. 3, 21). If we have attained to this, God will be the Alpha and Omega of all earthly things, the beginning and the end, and we shall see Him present in all things; and in many a circumstance of our own lives shall venture reverently to say, "God hath sent His angel" and saved me from this danger, or given me this happiness; and to Him I commit myself, and am prepared in all things to say, "Lord, undertake for me;" and "to Thy name be the glory for ever, Amen."

XXII.

RIGHTEOUS RETRIBUTION.

(DANIEL vi. 22–28.)

WE have already seen that in ascribing his deliverance from the mouths of the lions to an angel sent by God, Daniel professes his faith in the active intervention of God in the affairs of men. And this belief separates the religious from the irreligious. Call him by what name you will, the irreligious man is one whose life has no higher principle than such as grows out of human nature itself. Juvenal in old time summed up the philosophy of irreligion in the words, "Nullum numen adest si sit prudentia rerum:" "You may dispense with a deity if you manage your affairs with prudence." Good sense was his deity; in our days it is fixity of rule, the reign of laws unchanging alike in Nature and in the moral world; and all that the wise man has to do is to bring his conduct into accord with this fixed and unalterable mechanism which is ever grinding onward in its dull, unintelligent way. The Bible from first to last is a revelation of God's active, personal, and intelligent presence in the affairs of men; and its elementary principles, without which all approach to God is impossible, are, first, that there is a God, and secondly, that He rewards and punishes (Heb. xi. 6).

Take away the presence of God, and we can find no reason for man's existence. He becomes the mere plaything of Nature, the chance product of a machine without a mechanist, which, devoid of sense and reason, is ever "evolving" something higher and higher, though why it should do so, and how it began this process, and what is the purpose of its evolution, no one can even guess. That very wise law called "the survival of the fittest," which provides for constant improvement —for the removal of the bad and commonplace, and the substitution of the better—is, we are told, the mere result of an arrangement of atoms which came into existence no one knows how, and which, without intelligent will and conscious purpose, moves onward to no definite or intended result, though somehow or other it always manages to arrange itself better and better. What will happen when nothing exists but the one thing fittest to survive everything else no one can tell us, because the conclusion is so infinitely absurd. Possibly the machine will evolve back again, and produce that which is worse. But when man's place is taken by some result of evolution as much superior to man as he is to his simian progenitors, this noble creature will be just as much without a reason for his existence as man is now. If the question be asked, Whence he came? the sole answer would be that he has been developed out of the dust of the earth by some unknown force acting upon him through countless ages. If you ask Why? For what purpose or intent? there is no answer. The oracle of physical science is as dumb or ambiguous as that of the Delphian Apollo.

The Bible sets man before us as having his origin in God, and as moving onwards towards God. And throughout its pages it shows us a higher power than that either of Nature or of man actively present in the world, and always making for right and truth. And in God man finds his explanation, and the world its use. Man is placed here that he may struggle onwards to peace and happiness and perfection in God. And to aid him in the effort required for his upward course a wonderful scheme of redemption has been divinely made known to him, such as especially warms his affections and draws his heart towards the Deity, known to him no longer as the Author and Ruler of Nature, but as a loving Father, who saves His people from sin and danger through the gift of His Son, Jesus Christ our Lord.

Daniel recognised the presence of this Divine power when he said that "God had sent His angel, and shut the lions' mouths." Left to their natural instincts these fierce beasts would have torn Daniel to pieces, and feasted upon his remains. They would have been forced to do this by the law of their being; but the reign of law had in this case been broken. Something higher and more mighty than Nature had intervened, and had overpowered their indomitable instincts. Daniel felt no doubt as to whose this power was. A message had come to the lions from God, and they perforce must obey. The same thing may happen now, though we call it simply providence. But providence means forethought; that God cares for men, and so regulates the inferior powers of Nature and human conduct as is best for the spiritual interests of His people. The sole difference between miracle and providence is, that in the former case the ordinary laws of Nature are suspended and interfered with by the higher power; in the latter Nature is made to do the will of God in conformity with its usual way of working. And these two ways of acting have had each a suitableness for the times when God used them. Miracle and prophecy had a special value before the scheme of redemption was complete, because they arrested men's attention, and upon fit occasions gave them, as it were by force, the evidence necessary to produce the conviction of God's active and personal rule over men and the world. They have great teaching power now, and attested as they are both by sound reason and adequate proof, they are sufficient to maintain in thoughtful minds the required belief in those fundamental principles required as indispensable for every one who comes unto God (Heb. xi. 6). With the whole plan of redemption made known to us, and God's revelation complete, such startling events as miracles would now be out of place. They were a compensation in old time for the partial light then vouchsafed; as wrought by our Lord, they were the necessary effects of His divinity; for us there is the full light of revelation, the full teaching of Him who is "the Light." We have what is sufficient, and the extraordinary help given occasionally in old time would interfere with the salutary and adequate influences which are so richly granted to us. But God is equally present with His people now, only He orders all things for them by His providence, and leads them by gentle guidance and ordinary help to their final home in that world which is the consummation of this lower existence. But a providential deliverance is as real an intervention of God as one miraculous, and St. Paul acknowledged no difference of kind between his deliverance from the Emperor Nero and that of Daniel (2 Tim. iv. 17).

The reason of this deliverance Daniel finds in the just government of God. He was doubly innocent, for he had not been remiss or negligent in his duty to God, and as regards the king, this anxious visit of Darius in the early morning to the lions' den was proof enough that he acquitted his minister of all offence. God, therefore, as the just Ruler of the world, had protected Daniel from all harm, and had done so by a miraculous intervention. But the intervention is no less real when God saves men without a miracle. When a Christian asserts, in the Psalmist's words, that "the angel of the Lord encampeth round about them that fear God, and delivereth them" (Ps. xxxiv. 7), it is not only the expression of firm faith, but is his testimony to a fact. For in the history of his past life he finds frequent occasions on which his prayers have been answered, and deliverance vouchsafed.

"Then was the king exceeding glad for him, and commanded that they should take Daniel up out of the den. So Daniel was taken up out of the den, and no manner of hurt was found upon him, because he believed in his God (ver. 23).

The joy of the king was in proportion to the sorrow which had made him pass the night watchful and fasting. And, moreover, the extraordinary way of Daniel's deliverance would increase his happiness, for it was proof both of innocence and of Divine favour. It was the attestation of Heaven that the minister so faithful to him was greatly beloved of God. But most worthy of our attention is the reason given for an event so contrary to ordinary experience. When Daniel was cast into the lions' den, looking so old and feeble, so unfit physically to cope with those fierce wild beasts, there was, nevertheless, present in his heart a power that can remove mountains. That power was faith. The king had some small hope, but it was as nothing compared with the fears and doubts which filled his mind. Daniel had no fear nor doubt. He knew in whom he had believed, and that night passed among the lions was one of quiet and sweet confidence. And how great the contrast! The king is sick at heart, miserable and careworn amid all his regal splendour; while happiness and peace and contentment are bestowed upon the man whose lot we should call so terrible, and who had been brought by malignant enemies to so cruel a fate. Happiness does not depend upon outward circumstances, but upon the heart; and Daniel enjoyed it " because he believed in his God."

"And the king commanded, and they brought those men which had accused Daniel, and they cast them into the den of lions, them, their children, and their wives; and the lions had the mastery of them, and brake all their bones in pieces or ever they came at the bottom of the den" (ver. 24).

It was a fearful retribution. They had digged a pit and fallen into the midst of it themselves. With cool forethought and premeditation they had plotted the murder of the chief minister of the realm; and in his wonderful preservation both the king and all who had not shared in the crime saw emphatic proof of the guilt of the conspirators. Their own execution was most just, but our feelings revolt at the inclusion in the sentence of their wives and children; but it was the Persian custom, and may have grown out of the feeling generally prevalent in old time, that the son was bound to avenge the shedding of the father's blood. To spare the children was thus to leave a crop of blood-feuds. But the sense of the sacredness of human life is the slow result of Christian teaching, while it is a debt which we owe to the Romans that no man should be condemned without being allowed to speak for himself. Respect for law was the great lesson which the Romans were employed to teach mankind. Among the Persians and many other ancient nations, justice rose no higher than retaliation. It was public and authorised revenge. And in this wholesale execution the people in those days would see only a cause for rejoicing. It was right triumphing over wrong, and they would have no scruples about including those personally innocent.

There is, too, another side in this solidarity of interest between the members of the same family or of the same nation. The sins of one member of a family often involve all in ruin. A whole nation has to pay the penalty of the fault of its statesmen; a whole army is destroyed by the incapacity of its general. But equally all share in the results of the virtues, the wisdom, the ability of their leaders, and it would be a poor world if it were not so. In the Old Testament this close union of men in families and states, and their responsibility for one another's conduct, is put as prominently forward as our personal responsibility to God each for our own conduct is taught in the New Testament. Not that men were not warned of this by God in old time. Ezekiel especially (see chap. xviii.) was commissioned to correct the one-sided appreciation by the people of the former truth, and bring out its other side into due prominence. To the Persians a man's wives and children were one with himself, and must share his lot. The same feeling made it the law with the Hindus for the wife to share the husband's funeral pile. They were cruel and abominable exaggerations of a right fundamental principle; but a wife and children starved or brutalised by the drunkenness of a husband is a thing quite as revolting, and the education of the community in Christian feeling has not advanced far as long as such a crime is possible among us. As for the number of those put to death, the conspiracy was probably confined to Daniel's two fellow-presidents and their immediate followers. It was a powerful court intrigue, but did not extend beyond the chiefs and nobles in attendance upon the king's person.

"Then king Darius wrote unto all people (the peoples, R. V.), nations, and languages, that dwell in all the earth; Peace be multiplied unto you. I make a decree, that in every dominion of my kingdom men tremble and fear before the God of Daniel: for He is the living God, and steadfast for ever, and His kingdom that which shall not be destroyed, and His dominion shall be even unto the end. He delivereth and rescueth, and He worketh signs and wonders in heaven and in earth, who hath delivered Daniel from the power of the lions" (vers. 25–27).

In making this proclamation, Darius was following the custom of Nebuchadnezzar and other Oriental monarchs, who from time to time took their subjects into their confidence, and made them acquainted with events of more than common importance. We owe to this custom the inscriptions upon rocks, and the records upon the Assyrian tablets, which preserve for us such valuable facts of history. When printing was introduced, monarchs published their messages in gazettes, and it is now the office of newspapers and journals to keep the people informed of all matters of local or general interest. Darius made known what had happened by a special decree, and this is a proof to us of the importance he attached to it, as only events of extraordinary interest would be deemed worthy of so special a record.

It has been noticed that the decree is not so truculent as that of Nebuchadnezzar, who threatened to cut men in pieces and make their houses a dunghill if they spake words of disparagement of the God of Shadrach (chap. iii. 29). It is much more in the spirit of chap. iv., which is the expression of

Nebuchadnezzar's thankfulness to the God of Daniel for mercies received. But these edicts had a higher use than the mere recording of a monarch's gratitude. The Jews held a special position upon the earth as the representatives of the unity of the Godhead, and as the keepers of the inspired oracles (Rom. iii. 2). But the glory of their realm had departed. The empire of David, the wisdom and splendour of Solomon, had given place to two petty realms ever weakened by their own dissensions, and finally trampled under foot by the boot of the Assyrian. How could the crushed remnant of this small people, itself daily more and more absorbed in the world's trade and merchandise, discharge its special function? Their wonderful genius for commerce made them an important element in every great city, and so gave them a post of vantage everywhere, and special opportunities. But commerce was no more sanctified to God then than is British commerce now, and the Jewish trader was in danger of forgetting that he had a mission for mankind. Depressed therefore by national misfortune, and debased by a multitude of petty cares, the people of Jehovah seemed only too likely to waste away and be lost in the vast heathen world which had so tightly enveloped them. It was not without a purpose, therefore, that again and again there pealed forth from the centre of government a summons to respect and reverence the Jewish God. Twice did the haughty Nebuchadnezzar acknowledge that Jehovah was more mighty than any earthly throne or empire. And when his kingdom had fallen before the conquering Medes and Persians, again sounds forth the homage to the God of Daniel, the living God, the God true and steadfast, and whose dominion is everlasting. And Darius claims to speak as the head of the whole habitable world. His proclamation is addressed to all the peoples, nations, and languages that dwell in all the earth. He was claiming more than he had a right to geographically; but morally and providentially he was the earth's monarch, and the supreme governor of the second world-power. It was thus the homage paid by the habitable world through its king to the Jehovah of Israel, and it acknowledged Him as a Being of higher and more Divine attributes than any of the gods of the heathen nations. There was in this more than a compensation for the loss of national independence and military achievement. The Jew began to learn that his God was his strength, and slowly and surely they were formed into a people of missionaries, whose office it was to bear far and wide God's truth.

We often wonder at the tenacity of the Jews, at their firmness and heroism, and their extraordinary power of bearing all kinds of calamities and surviving them. Perhaps we do not wonder so much as we ought at twelve Galilean fishermen being fit to evangelise the world. If the highly educated and gifted Paul laboured more abundantly than they all, yet the highest products of a nation always stand in relation to the general average. And if we except St. Paul's indefatigable activity and his largeness of view, he does not surpass either a Peter or a John; and they, too, have their special excellences. Now national qualities do not come by chance. They are slowly formed, and chiefly so by mental influences. The Jews were formed to be God's missionaries by their prophets, and when prophecy ceased then came these wonderful events at Babylon, and then the Maccabees. The Jewish is a wonderful history, forming a wonderful people; and these three decrees coming one after another, and speaking especially to the heart of the Jews, raised them up from their depression, and made them bold both to do and to speak for God.

Wonderful, therefore, as are the events recorded in the Book of Daniel, they were not without their justification. God does not work "signs and wonders in heaven and in earth" without a purpose;

and Daniel was raised up, and had so extraordinary a history, and was again and again so marvellously rescued, as part of that special training required by and given to the Jews as the destined missionaries of our blessed Lord.

And is there no purpose in their special preservation and training now? Yes, verily, God never works in vain; and we know that all Israel is to be saved (Rom. xi. 26); and that the receiving of them into the Church will be to the Gentile world like life from the dead (ibid. 15).

"So this Daniel prospered in the reign of Darius, and in the reign of Cyrus the Persian" (ver. 28).

His special work was done, and God granted his faithful servant a calm and peaceful close to his chequered career. He had seen many monarchs come and go. He had been hurried as a child from the devastated homes of the kings of Judah, his ancestors. He had attained to high rank in the court of the conqueror, and outlived him. He had passed through the troubled times of murder and anarchy which followed, and again had been brought out of obscurity to be the central figure in the strange scenes which brought the Babylonian monarchy to an abrupt end. In the court of the conquerors his merit had raised him to the foremost place, and then came a fearful proving in the fiery furnace of trial. But innocency was found in him both toward God and man. Henceforward there was the calm, peaceful eventide of life, with its warm brilliance and steady glow of light and golden sunshine, fit harbinger for the prophet of the resurrection of that awakening, when "the wise shall shine as the brightness of the firmament; and they that turn many to righteousness as the stars for ever and ever" (chap. xii. 3).

And step by step we have followed him from the day when as a handsome youth he stood before Melzar, and in what must have seemed to the old steward mere childish enthusiasm, petitioned that he and his boy friends might have pulse and water for their food instead of the wine and dainties sent them from the king. We have seen him grow in knowledge and power, until he became the chief minister of the mighty despot who was the golden head of the first universal monarchy, and then of the conqueror who had crushed that empire to the dust. And from first to last there was the same simple piety, the same unswerving obedience to the dictates of his conscience, the same unwavering trust in God as had marked his youthful years.

Power had no corrupting influence over him, nor did he as he grew unto worldly greatness, fall away from his early virtue, but on the contrary ever walked nearer unto God, and increased in faith and holiness. In following this noble life we have endeavoured to draw from it some of the many morals it contains. The incidents recorded are startling and extraordinary, but not without a reason. Daniel lived at a time when the chosen people seemed doomed to destruction, and their work to failure. He saved them; under God's good providence he made them more fit to carry on their appointed work. Had we in our wisdom had the ordering of events, we should have given the chosen people a grand empire, faultless kings, an intense appreciation of the holiness of their work, great opportunities for good. God gave them the exact reverse; but His training made Galilean fishermen fit apostles for the Lord, and the Jews generally able to comprehend and preach the pure truths of the Gospel. In this training Daniel was a great factor. Our object has been to gather from his life such lessons as may aid us in walking worthily of that high vocation which we have inherited from the Jews; only we possess the truth in its perfection and fulness, while they had it as it was gradually revealed, "in many portions and divers ways." If any of God's people are aided and strengthened in the Christian life by any words we have written, our object will have been attained; and to God be the glory. Amen.

THE END.

www.ingramcontent.com/pod-product-compliance
Lightning Source LLC
Chambersburg PA
CBHW032048220426
43664CB00008B/915